Don't Read My Lips!

America's Foremost Female Ventriloquist Reveals the Secrets of How to be a Successful Vent

APRIL BRUCKER

Library of Congress Control Number: 2021934715

ISBN-10: 0-9842085-8-5
ISBN-13: 978-0-9842085-8-6

Publisher: CFBP Bestsellers
An imprint of CFB Productions LLC
P.O. Box 50008, Henderson, NV 89016
www.CFBPBestsellers.com

DEDICATION

To my biggest fan, Anne Brucker, my mom. When I told you that I wanted to make people laugh and make puppets talk, you didn't tell me no. Instead, you said, "Baby, we need to get you to New York."

CONTENTS

Charlie McCarthy
& Egdar Bergen
inspired my
adVENTure!

ACKNOWLEDGMENTS

This book would not have been possible without the ancient art of ventriloquism and every ventriloquist out there in the world. In my adventures, I have met vents not only from across the USA, but from around the globe, whether it be Argentina, Brazil, India, Morocco, Singapore, Turkey or Nigeria — just to name a few places. While we might not all speak English, the need to make puppets talk connects us all. I am pleased to report ventriloquism isn't simply surviving, but thriving.

I would like to talk about all the vents who inspired me. These include, but are not limited to, Ray Allen, Edgar Bergen, Nina Conti, Jeff Dunham, Shari Lewis, Otto Petersen, Willie Tyler and Paul Winchell. I cannot tell you how many late nights I watched your videos on YouTube or your television specials and I am still floored by your innovative genius.

I also want to note that I did get to work with Otto Petersen towards the end of his life. Not only did this late-great show me how to be a better ventriloquist and comedian onstage, but how to be a class act offstage too.

A very special thank you to Steve Axtell, Nigel 'Docta Gel' Dunkley, Conrad Hartz, Steve Hewlett, Jay Johnson, Taylor Mason and Mark Wade for letting me interview you for this book. I have long since admired your work as vents, teachers and figure makers. Being able to talk about vent with you was a once in a lifetime experience. You made my research for this book a true learning experience and your love and knowledge for ventriloquism was both humbling and enlivening.

I would be remiss if I didn't mention my manager, Clinton Ford Billups Jr., who for some time now has been trying to get me to write a book about ventriloquism. Right now, you are making Clinton happy as your purchase has earned him a commission.

Shout out to my Aubergine cohort. We graduated Antioch University together with our MFA's in Creative Writing. Not only do you all watch me on television and follow me online, but you are with me in spirit every time I write anything, anywhere, and for any reason.

To my father, brother, sister, brother-in-law, sister-in-law, aunts, uncles and cousins, thank you for putting up with my need to make puppets talk. While having me around wasn't always easy, you all nonetheless attended my shows and events, plus never missed any of my TV appearances.

Shout out to these NYC venues: Arno's, Broadway Comedy Club, Don't Tell Mama, The Duplex, The Metropolitan

Room, New York Comedy Club, The People's Improv Theatre, Standup NY, The Stonewall and The Triple Crown. Thank you for giving May Wilson and me stage time early on, but also for making us feel at home.

Special thank you to Dave Cable, Rich Carucci, the late Scott Gray, David Marcus and Tony Vitali for believing in my puppets and I when many people did not.

Finally, to my puppet children, especially May Wilson. You are not only the driving force behind what keeps me going, but you make me look good anytime we do anything anywhere.

Storytime
with April
& Friends
My first TV
adVENTure
was on
Public Access
Taping for
"My Strange
Addiction"
on TLC

INTRODUCTION

YOU: Who are you?

ME: I'm a ventriloquist.

YOU: How did you become a ventriloquist?

ME: It was a dark and stormy night in Bethel Park, PA. I was thirteen, awkward, and sitting in my family TV room after my brother's high school football game as we did every Friday. What made this night different was we finally had cable. My parents (both educators) felt cable was unnecessary because we should be reading. However, we had been forced to get cable because they wanted to see scores from the neighboring school districts because we lived in Steeler County.

YOU: Okay, we get it. You were weird and had no friends. Now get to the part where you become a ventriloquist?

ME: My dad hated commercials. So, when he changed the channel, there was an Edgar Bergen tribute show.

YOU: Okay, what's an Edgar Bergen?

ME: Edgar Bergen was a famous ventriloquist and his figure's name was Charlie McCarthy. Anyway, my whole family tried to talk like the ventriloquists on the TV, but because I inherited my great-grandmother's sideways Irish smile, I was the only one who could do it. That Christmas, my mom put a Groucho Marx figure under the tree.

YOU: So that Christmas, when you picked up that Groucho Marx, you became an awesome ventriloquist?

ME: No, grasshopper. I had to work hard, very hard. I had to learn proper technique, lip control, how to create a character, how to write a joke, how to create dialogue and how to market myself. That is what I am going to teach you in this book. Want to learn how to make puppets talk? Want me to tell you everything I learned from the greats before me, like Shari Lewis, the first prominent female vent on television?

YOU: Maybe, but why are we talking in dialogue.

ME: Cause I just made you my puppet and now I am in control. So now that I am pulling your strings, you are going to turn the page.

Cheers,

April Brucker

April Brucker
www.AprilBrucker.TV

A big hit in
London's
music halls!
JAMES BURNS,
or Squeaking Tommy,
A well known VENTRILOQUIST through the County of Nottingham;
Died January 7th 1796.
Pubd. July 31. 1804. by R. S. Kirby. London House Yard & J. Scott 447. Strand.

1 THE HISTORY OF VENTRILOQUISM

In ancient Greece at the Temple of Apollo, there was a group of high priestesses called The Pythia who comprised The Oracle of Delphi. People came from near and far to get their fortunes told, because it was believed whatever the oracle said would come to fruition.

When The Oracle would reveal a prophesy, a wall of thick white smoke would rise, and The Oracle would speak in gibberish. After the person seeking The Oracle's wisdom unscrambled the message, the prediction was revealed.

As they received their fate, The Oracle's voice came from a strange distance that was hard to place. No one quite knew where The Oracle was exactly, which added to this glorious wonder of the Hellenic realm.

One such wisdom seeker was beautiful young Queen Jocasta and her handsome husband, King Laius. Both rulers, who presided over the plague-ridden kingdom of Thebes, wanted to know the future of their empire. Holding her infant son,

Jocasta hoped his birth would end the famine.

Unfortunately, The Oracle had other plans, "Your son will grow up to kill his father and marry his mother." Upon hearing this, Laius ordered Jocasta to kill their son. Unable to harm her infant, Jocasta ordered a servant to do the deed. Taking pity upon the young child, the servant instead gave the infant to some shepherds for safe keeping. The shepherds, good subjects, left the baby with King Polybus, whose wife had wanted for a child for so long. They named the boy Oedipus.

Oedipus grew up to be a strapping lad who liked chariot racing. One day as he was racing down the street, he encountered an old man named Laius and his servants. There was an argument over who had the right of way. Both had some serious chariot rage and Laius tried to hit Oedipus with his walking stick. In return, Oedipus struck Laius killing him. (Never a traffic cop around when you need one.) After solving the riddle of the Spynx (at least he wasn't chariot racing), he married Jocasta. As you can guess, it didn't end well; Google it.

This bizarre tale of Oedipus has fascinated psychologists and academics for centuries. What does this have to do with my book? Answer: The Oracle of Delphi was the first ventriloquist! (When interviewed, a publicist for The Oracle said, "While we cannot comment on that incident, visitors are now required to sign a waiver absolving us of all legal responsibility.")

Ventriloquism comes from two Latin words, venter (belly), and loqui (speak). So, when one is a ventriloquist, one is a belly speaker. While The Oracle of Delphi is the first representation in literature, there are real life documentations of those practicing ventriloquism in the ancient world for the purpose of channeling the beyond. (So much for trying to dispel the scary movie stereotype.)

The Zulu people of Africa as well as the Maori of Australia and New Zealand believed that the souls of the deceased resided in a person's stomach. Those who could throw their voices in these cultures were regarded as highly sought out mediums and their gift was often showcased in ceremonies where attendees wanted to commune with those who passed on. (While Yelp wasn't yet invented, by all surviving accounts, their customers were happier than those who visited The Oracle of Delphi.)

For centuries, ventriloquism continued to be spiritual, mystical and religious, but in the mid-1700s it took on a different shape: Entertainment. In 1754, William Hogarth, an Irish humorist, published a cartoon in which Northern Irish Protestant land owning baron Sir John Parnell was lampooned as having a lively conversation with his hand. This work of art inspired Jonathan Swift and his satire, but historians speculate the inspiration was a ventriloquist Hogarth encountered in his countryside travels.

Meanwhile, in Austria, arts patron and known eccentric Baron de Mengen began to carry around "a small baby doll" whose mouth did not move. The Baron not only carried his inanimate companion everywhere he went, but used his sidekick to express himself when he felt uncomfortable. Soon The Baron graduated to parlor shows for his friends and family members. While this audience was amused, they regarded him as yet another ridiculous royal. Now we know better, The Baron was just practicing his ventriloquism.

The art of ventriloquism soon made its way off of the pages of political satire, out of The Baron's parlor and into the comedy music halls of London. Of these early music hall vents was most notably James Burne, commonly called Squeaking Tommy, whose companion was noted as being, "an ill-shaped doll, with a board face….and he exhibits an utterance of childish jargon." (It should be noted that the "doll" in question refused to be interviewed for this book, wanted to remain anonymous and was rather insulted at his physical description.)

Early ventriloquism was not just limited to "dolls." Swiss ventriloquist Louis Comte performed a travelling show with a cast of pigs. Comte made the pigs talk and each had a distinct voice and personality. A hit with audiences, Louis Comte was soon touring Europe. (A representative for the pigs said, "We did all the work, hamming it up and bringing home the bacon. In exchange we got peanuts. We are pigs, not elephants.")

In France, Alexandre Vattemare, a magician and quick change artist whose stage name was Monsieur Alexandre, gained significant publicity when he performed an act in cemeteries where the deceased called to him from the ground. It should be noted one macabre reason for the success of Vattemare's act was during this period in history, it was not uncommon for people to be accidentally buried alive. Many cemeteries had bells which one could ring if they "woke up," therefore being rescued before they suffocated.

In Vattemare's act, those who were "waking up" were heard from below. This marvelous-mimicking, ventriloquism-practicing, voice-throwing virtuoso was so convincing that it appeared as if the departed were conversing with Vattemare. The act became so legendary that a book detailing his exploits was published entitled *The Rogueries of Nicholas.* (A living-impaired person whom Vattemare played said, "Gotta hand it to him, his impression of me was dead on. I'd cadaver to know how he knew so much about me.")

Ventriloquism soon made its way from Europe to the United States through magician Richard Potter, inventor of the Hindu Rope trick. A black performer, Potter was more often than not discriminated against because of the color of his skin in pre-Civil War America. The addition of a "wooden doll" gained him fame, helping to draw crowds from all around making him what is regarded as the first African American celebrity. Potter would go on to inspire the character of Richard Peyton in the drama *Peyton Place.* (His "wooden doll," who's writing a tell-all memoir, is incredulous that he was not cast as Richard Peyton.)

The first ventriloquist to achieve international stardom was British vent Fred Russell, OBE. Russell and his puppet pal, Coster Joe, a cheeky boy who had smart-mouthed retorts to his master, were a hit with audiences. The two were so popular they had a permanent engagement at The Palace Theatre in London. A plaque there still reads, "Fred Russell, the Father of Modern Ventriloquism, lived here." (Coster Joe had only one comment: "Good for him. He died and now I'm unemployed.")

Ventriloquists soon graduated from music halls to the vaudeville circuit and the burlesque stages. The art form grew and so did the number of vents performing. This meant not only did the number of vents become more visible and widespread, but it meant that the art form was being passed on. Some of these vents not only were achieving success as practitioners, but also as teachers.

The most legendary of these pedagogues was The Great Lester. With wooden partner, Frank Byron Jr., Lester shined on the vaudeville circuit, not only walking through the audience while Frank whistled, but also perfecting the effect of drinking water as Frank spoke. When not performing, Lester began conducting weekly sessions with fledgling would-be ventriloquists who dreamed of a life trodding the boards.

Lester, who gave his students breathing and articulation exercises, encouraged them to tape record their progress. His methods gave birth to many modern ventriloquism courses, such as *The Maher Studios Pamphlet.* (In case you are wondering about Frank Byron Jr., he retired after Lester passed away. You can visit him at the Vent Haven Museum in Fort Mitchell, Kentucky.)

While Lester had many who wanted to learn vent under his esteemed tutelage, the most famous of his pupils was a young man named Edgar Bergen. With a brood that contained Charlie McCarthy, Mortimer Snerd and Effie Klinker, Bergen became the seminal ventriloquist superstar of the Golden Age of Hollywood.

Edgar Bergen and Charlie McCarthy made successful film appearances, but also had the top-rated radio program of the 1940s, *The Charlie McCarthy Radio Hour*. Celebrities, including The Andrews Sisters, WC Fields, Frank Sinatra, Groucho Marx, Mae West and many others, performed with Edgar and Charlie. The duo would go on to make an iconic appearance in *The Muppet Movie*.

Edgar and Charlie gave birth to Paul Winchell and Jerry Mahoney, Jimmy Nelson and Danny O'Day, Willie Tyler and Lester, Shari Lewis and Lambchop, Jeff Dunham and his crew and the list goes on.

Due to the dedication and success of these early pioneers and the Internet, people from around the world can not only watch ventriloquism, but have access to learn the art form, too. This global diversity can be seen each year at Vent Haven ConVENTion.

Held annually at The Holiday Inn Cincinnati Airport Hotel, there are also shuttles to the Vent Haven Museum in Fort Mitchell, Kentucky, where vents of today can learn about the generation of vents before them. Memorabilia includes, but is not limited to, classic vent figures, playbills and everything in between.

ConVENTion attracts vents of all levels, from the beginner and the seasoned pro to celebrities, such as Jeff Dunham and Jay Johnson. Each year, there are workshops, showcases, dealer's tables and other opportunities to perfect one's craft and network. Director Mark Wade, who terms this gathering "a family reunion," estimates that at least 181 countries are represented.

What does it take to be the next great ventriloquist? Hard work, talent, passion, dedication and a great imagination. Who will be that vent? Maybe it will be you. How can you be that vent? I'll tell you if you turn the page (after you check out one of several anecdotes that I'll share with you throughout the book).

An April Anecdote

When we were mere comedy neophytes, May Wilson and I appeared on the *Rachael Ray* television show in a segment entitled "Audience Has Talent." Jerry Springer, who at the time was not only the reigning King of Trash TV, but was also host of *America's Got Talent*, was appearing on Rachel's show as a special guest judge.

May Wilson and I went onstage in front of the studio audience to do our act. We were hoping to get discovered, win the grand prize of $1,000 and to get an audition with the producers of *America's Got Talent*. This was going to be our big break.

Then Jerry Springer gave us the big "X." Jerry said, "Sorry, but you are no Terry Fator." The verdict was as harsh as a fight on his tawdry show. However, I used that moment not only to make me a better ventriloquist, but also to drive me harder to someday get my own show in Las Vegas.

Fast forward. Terry Fator's Vegas residency at The Mirage ended in mid-2020. From December 2020 to August 2021, May Wilson and I headlined as the special guest stars in *BurlesQ*, an all-female, classic Vegas revue, and I was the only ventriloquist performing in The City of Entertainment. So, to Jerry Springer, "You were right. I am no Terry Fator."

My Mom and
her puppet
Patty
Perkins

2 WHY LEARN VENTRILOQUISM

A lot of you may have been drawn to this book because you want to be a professional ventriloquist. That is fabulous news. As a professional ventriloquist myself, I have been lots of places, met a lot of people and have had a life beyond my wildest dreams. So, if you want to get on this whacky ride with us showbiz folks, come aboard; the train could use more starry-eyed passengers with tremendous imaginations.

However, maybe you have no intention of becoming a professional ventriloquist and picked up this book because you are curious and just always wanted to learn. The good news is: That's okay. I will be the first to acknowledge that while my chosen profession is not for everyone, learning the art form is.

Even if you don't want a career in showbiz, learning vent is still a worthwhile pursuit. It's a fun fact about yourself to put on a college application, a cool thing to check off the bucket list or a ready-made prop for an office presentation.

Perhaps you are passionate about learning vent, but work a nine-to-five job with overhead and commitments. Maybe you are open to where the journey takes you, but don't want to go full-time straight away. Congratulations, you are sane and logical.

That being said, a great many vents do this as a pastime. Known as hobbyists in the vent world, some hobbyists never take their act outside of the walls of their house. Others perform for free at local church functions, community days or VFW halls. Then there are those who "do it on the side," receiving some money for their services, but not enough to quit their full time gig. If this is the type of vent you want to be, there is plenty of room for you in the ventriloquist community. According to Mark Wade, hobbyists make up a significant portion of the ConVENTioneers at Vent Haven.

It is not uncommon for a hobbyist to be employed in a field such as education. There has been many a hobbyist teacher that has done a puppetry unit with their classes and introduced the basics of ventriloquism to school-age kids. In passing vent along, these hobbyists perhaps gave a shy struggling child an outlet for expression. Not only did the youngster take to vent, but perhaps partly because of this hobbyist that little vent-in-training might grow into the next big name in our world.

Then there are those hobbyist teachers who go a step further in the classroom using ventriloquism as an educational tool. Pupils not only get a laugh and a show, but the lesson registers for a lifetime. Ventriloquism has been used to teach math, science, reading, English and history.

Outside of the core academic subjects, vent also has been used to teach important life skills. Steve Axtell, a veteran figure maker says, "I have had fire departments contact me to make a puppet in order to teach children about how to call 9-1-1." Not only have the youngsters enjoyed the entertaining character, but now know when and why to call the police, paramedics or fire department.

Some teachers find great success in using ventriloquism for classroom management, such as ConVENtion director Mark Wade. A teacher for many years, Mark rewarded his classes with his entertaining vent act if they behaved and their work was done. "If they were good, they got the show."

Ultimately, Mark left the classroom, became a full-time ventriloquist and is now the number one kid's vent in the country. However, he still uses his expertise to conduct audience management workshops at ConVENTion for anyone seeking to use vent with young people in any setting whether it's performers who want to entertain young audiences, classroom teachers, Sunday school teachers or youth ministers. Not only do these workshops emphasize the importance of putting on a good presentation, but how to do so for an audience with developing minds.

Ventriloquism also can be used to teach adolescent and young adult audiences about more serious subjects. I myself have used ventriloquism in my community outreach and activism to teach young people about anti-cyberbullying, homophobia/transphobia, HIV/AIDS awareness, domestic violence prevention and sexual awareness/consent. Not only does the puppet help add levity, but it helps have a serious conversation with young people who are at risk.

Doctors also have used ventriloquism to educate their elderly patients about nutrition and diabetes. My sister, Dr. Brenna Brucker, while at Brown University Medical School, had a puppet named Dr. Know-It-All. Brenna and Dr. Know-It-All answered questions about diet, exercise and any other health issues that her patients over 65 had. Not only were they a hit, but their audiences felt safe and informed. (Like many a great comedy duos, Brenna and Dr. Know-It-All later broke up. Dr. Know-It-All wanted to stay in Providence, RI, but Brenna wanted to take a job in Columbia, SC, where it was warm. Alas, all good things must come to an end.)

Vent also has been used to educate people of all age groups about aquatic safety. My mom, Anne Brucker, who would later go on to become The Most Valuable Female Athlete in swimming and The Most Valuable Woman in Education at The University of Pittsburgh, helped financed her undergraduate degree by teaching campers of all ages aquatic safety with her puppet partner, Patty Perkins. Dressed in a Girl Scout uniform matching my mom's, Patty not only helped answer questions, but people who could not swim or were scared of the water for any reason, could talk about their fears. Patty helped the campers learn about life jackets and CPR, but was such a hit she began to play a double engagement telling scary stories by the campfire at night. (Patty is now a recluse, living in my mother's attic. When asked to comment she said, "The whole family makes dolls talk. The horror! The horror!")

Social workers, psychologists and those in the mental health field have found vent as a wonderful tool to get people to open up about trauma. Many who counsel children, especially who have been subject to parents experiencing a tumultuous divorce, physical abuse or sexual abuse, have witnessed their young clients opening up when speaking to a puppet. Being able to talk about their feelings to a puppet creates comfort and progress and paves the way for healing.

Vent also has been successful in helping children on the autism spectrum. Steve Axtell used vent as a part of his therapy practice in dealing with non-verbal children. He found not only did they like the puppets, but it gave them a way to express themselves that they did not previously have.

Ventriloquism also can be used as a tool to help children overcome learning disabilities as well as other self-esteem issues. Prior to picking up a puppet, Jay Johnson struggled with dyslexia and Nigel Dunkley with a stutter. For both men, ventriloquism gave them a form of expression and confidence that helped launch them into successful careers.

While ventriloquism is about putting on shows, it is also about educating, reaching people and giving a voice to those who might not have one. So, the question is why not learn ventriloquism?

My First Figure "Groucho"

3 YOUR FIRST VENTRILOQUIST FIGURE

Since you turned the page, it looks like you decided to learn ventriloquism. CONGRATULATIONS! You have the desire which is an important first step. Wanting to embark on this journey is HUGE! I couldn't be happier, and if the ventriloquists of the world were more organized, we would be throwing you a ticker tape parade.

Now it's time to get started. Here are the next three things you will need:

1. A good attitude.
2. A good work ethic.
3. A figure.

You might be wondering what is a figure? Figure is the industry term for "puppet" or "dummy." Note, in this book I will use the terms puppet and figure interchangeably, but my children prefer "Felt-American." (I refer to my puppets as my "children" and they refer to me as "Scary Puppet Lady.")

For those new to ventriloquism, you might be wondering what kind of figures there are, how much they cost and where to purchase them. Maybe you have been browsing online and have come across figure makers on Esty, stock figures on Amazon, or you might have even bided on eBay, but have no idea of what the particulars are of the make or model. Perhaps you might be on a limited budget. Whatever your quandary, this chapter is here to help.

Before we get into specific kinds of figures, if your means are limited, it is perfectly fine to work with a simple sock on your hand. Many a great vent, such as Taylor Mason, have started out with a simple sock. Shari Lewis's Lambchop had her humble beginnings as a sockette.

If you are going to use a sock, I suggest that you put eyes, nose, a mouth and maybe a hat on your friend to make them more real. (This is very important and we will talk about that later.)

If your financial means are limited and you don't want to use a sock, another household object is perfectly suitable. Jay Johnson and Jay Marshall made figures out of a tennis ball and glove respectively. Their figures came to life because not only are both men master ventriloquists, but the heart and soul they breathed into their creations. (Today, the tennis ball and Lefty, the glove, have a home in The Vent Haven Museum. Stop in and say hi.) If your creativity is pulling you that way, go for it.

In the event you want a proper figure on the lower cost end, a hand puppet is always a great option. Hand puppets can be found at outdoor markets, street fairs, magic stores or online shops. While many think of Mr. Garrison and his friend Mr. Hand, a lot of vents have had hand puppets as a part of their act, me included. (My very own Officer E and Sonny Jones are hand puppets. They have been seen on *The Layover, My Strange Addiction* and *Broke and Semi-Famous.*) Senor Wences's Paco, a frequent guest on *The Ed Sullivan Show*, also was a hand puppet.

The good thing about a hand puppet is that they are easy to transport because of their small size and light weight, fitting into a backpack or purse easily. However, it is also harder to see their mouths move, which can be a challenge if you are performing for a bigger crowd or on television. Hand puppets, because of their smaller sizes, are also less likely to have moving parts making them look less real. However, if you have enough talent and imagination you might well be able to overcome those obstacles.

Maybe as you are reading this, you want to get a puppet that is professionally designed, whether it is a stock character figure makers have on their websites or one that's custom-made to your specifications. You might want features that you feel are important like a certain look, hair color, moving eyes, ears and other parts, but want to know where to look for those figures.

Stock professional figures can be found online on Amazon, Etsy, VentriloquistSwapMeet or through the websites of figure makers. They can also be found at magic stores. You also can purchase these figures on the spot at The Dealer's Table at Vent Haven ConVENTion, where the figure maker is right there to answer any questions you might have.

If you want a figure that's custom-made for your use and is an original character that you want designed specifically, I suggest you seek out an independent figure maker though Etsy, ventriloquist Facebook groups or the Internet. At ConVENTion, you can also meet figure makers at The Dealer's Tables and inquire about your character and your needs.

In making a custom character, it is important to stay in constant contact with your figure maker, so that you are not only clear on what is going on, but you also are both happy in the end. Figure makers care a great deal about their creations, but are not mind readers. The more specifics you can give them for a custom character, the better. Will be the result. For instance, if you can give them photos and/or drawings of what you want, your creativity and their creativity can work better together.

If you choose to get a professional figure, whether a stock character or custom made, there are two types. The first is a Juro, or a wooden figure, otherwise known as a "dummy," such as Charlie McCarthy, Jerry Mahoney and Danny O'Day. Popular in the days of vaudeville and early television, many vents still work with Juro figures.

Wooden figures typically stand at least three feet tall, have a life-like body and have eyes and ears that move. In the back of their head is a trap door, which contains the spring that moves the mouth. On these figures, the head is removeable, and a switch on the pole below the head controls the mouth, eyes and ears.

Wooden figures, especially if they are being custom-made to order, start at $1800. Because of the intricacy of the design, the custom paint job, heavier weight and the fact they break more easily, wooden figures are less in demand than they once were. However, their realistic look still makes them a very sought after option.

A former Marine and graduate of Barnum and Bailey Clown College, Conrad Hartz has been making and performing with puppets for more than 50 years, whether marionettes or ventriloquist figures. Calling himself "The Last of the Mohicans," here are the tips Conrad gives vents interested in having a wooden figure:

1. Don't touch the face and don't let anyone else touch the face. It helps preserve the paint job as well as the face.
2. In the summertime, keep your figure in air conditioning. In the winter, keep your figure in the heat. This also helps preserve the paint job.
3. When you are done using your figure, put it back in the case so it doesn't get damaged.
4. Put socks over the hands and feet and a cloth over the face so these do not get damaged.

5. Sometimes the spring in the head breaks making the figure difficult to operate (an unfortunate hiccup with wooden figures). Mail it back to the figure maker and they will fix it, but keep the trap door in the back of the head easily accessible.

Many newbie vents, especially those having a custom wooden figure made, will want as many features as possible, feeling that this will make their figure better and therefore make them more successful in their pursuit of ventriloquial success. Conrad wisely advises against newer vents doing this, "Get a good act and everything will take care of itself."

I myself could not agree more. While a figure that works for you is key, there is no substitute for good character creation, technique and writing. No figure, no matter how well-crafted and how many extra features added, can make up for not having a routine.

The second kind of figure one can get is a soft mouth figure. Reminiscent of the Muppets, a soft mouth figure has bigger eyes, a bigger mouth, is lighter weight and is more visible on stage and television. A soft mouth figure is also much easier to store and transport.

Many traditionalists feel a drawback of soft mouth figures is they are not as expressive or authentic as their wooden counterparts. This couldn't be farther from the truth. In recent years, many soft mouth figure makers have started designing using latex, not only adding moving eyes and ears, but making the faces more malleable so the ventriloquist can use their fingers, giving their character more of a variety of facial expressions.

Another upside to the soft mouth puppet is that their bodies are easier to move. Figure makers such as Mary Ann Taylor (MAT Puppets and the maker of May Wilson) put strings on the bodies of the puppets, so the arms move whenever the head moves, making the character on your arm more animated.

Soft mouth puppets are also less expensive, starting at $500, depending on the maker, but costing more if you request a custom design. However, if your figure maker is using latex and you want a custom design, the puppet could cost as much as $5000.

While some are concerned that soft mouth puppets might be too small, this could be farther from the truth. They can be made at any size. Recently, I had a Joe Biden puppet, renamed Joe Bidentime, made by Smithsen Puppets. Not only is he easy to work and move, but he is also just as lifelike as his wooden comrades.

Just as many beginner vents want a wooden figure with a lot of features before they write an act, figure maker Steve Axtell echoes a warning similar to that of Conrad Hartz. He also has some homework that vents searching for the perfect puppet should do beforehand:

1. Start with the idea of knowing your own personality onstage.

2. Find a character that is the opposite of your personality. The routine writes itself.

Maybe you are reading this, have gotten to know the types of figures and have the means and desire to carve/make your own. Go for it. Jeff Dunham carved many of his early figures from scratch and wooden figure maker Conrad Hartz got started by making his own too. If you are going to go this route, Conrad advises you to be very patient and be very handy, because it will take longer than you think.

In making your own figure, you might discover you weren't as handy as you thought you were and abandon ship. (As someone who gets lost in Home Depot, I applaud you for trying.) However, you might also discover your niche. If this is the case, you could have a side business as a figure maker yourself. Not only will you be sought out in the vent community, but this lucrative income stream could also finance your own performing aspirations.

Perhaps you want a custom figure and are short on funds, but do not see yourself or your culture represented. In that case, it's okay to pre-purchase a figure and to augment it. As a young boy, Willie Tyler purchased a Jerry Mahoney, painted him black, gave him glasses and an Afro, and renamed him Lester. Willie and Lester have enjoyed a long career on television and stage and are still performing.

More recently, Nigel Dunkley got a hand puppet from a store, painted her black, put a wig on her and renamed her Cindy Hot Chocolate. When asked about being a black ventriloquist, he said, "It's cool. It's a way to see myself and people like me represented in the art form."

While there are people who are concerned these augmentations might destroy a puppet, these are farther from the truth. If anything, the original design gets a new dimension and your voice and culture are now part of the diverse fabric that weaves the international ventriloquist community together.

You might wonder what kind of figures I prefer. Well, I am partial to soft mouth puppets because of my small size, but I am also shopping the idea of a possible wooden figure for a future character to be revealed at a later date as I am a fool for nostalgia.

When looking for a figure, make sure it is one you can use in your act and can bring to life. And when creating a custom character for yourself, make sure it is one that is well thought out. Or, as Jay Johnson once warned me, "We all fall for pretty puppets."

So how do you make your partner that you are now performing with come alive? Answer, make them talk. That's what the next chapter is about.

Young April learning the art of Vent!

4 LEARNING TO BE A VENTRILOQUIST

You decided to get a figure. This is FABULOUS. Now here comes the good news and the bad news. Good News: You are about to have a lot of fun. Bad News: This is where the real hard work begins.

During this step, many newbie vents get intimidated and ultimately abandon their pursuit. Newsflash: Although making a puppet talk looks easy, ventriloquism is hard work. As Jay Johnson once explained to me, "Ventriloquism is an art form. Just as a musician has his cello, you have your puppet."

For this next step you will need four things:

1. A positive attitude.
2. A good work ethic.
3. Your figure.
4. A mirror.

You might want to video yourself on your cellphone to keep track of your progress, but don't play to the camera as if your recording device were an audience. Treat these sessions the way a professional athlete would treat practice tapes.

Now get in front of the mirror. You are welcome to sit or stand. In sitting, you are relaxed and your figure is on your knee. That way you are in a mental state where you can concentrate on the task at hand. Be forewarned though, the danger of sitting is your energy goes downward and ultimately drops.

If you stand, you are more engaged I find, but you will also find your figure suffers from the calamity known as "dead hang." This can be cured by putting your leg on a chair and balancing your figure on your knee, cradling your figure in your other hand so your figure does not hang limp or purchasing a puppet stool which can be done cheaply online. (Note, if you are handy, you can also make your own.)

A note about dead hang: It is a habit you need to nip in the bud immediately. If your figure dangles lifelessly, it not only is lazy ventriloquism, but it kills the illusion. Ventriloquism is all about the illusion and once the illusion is broken for any reason, you and your act, no matter how well crafted, will fail.

Before you get started, we need to talk about breathing. If you want to pursue ventriloquism, especially in a performance setting whether amateur or professional, it is important that you breathe and speak from your diaphragm. Not only will you have an easier time switching from your speaking voice and ventriloquial voice, but you will find that you are less likely to get a sore throat, especially if you are performing in a setting without a microphone.

A proper foundation for breathing techniques will help you fight frustration and anxiety, whether it is during your practice sessions, onstage or in life. We are not conditioned to breathe from the diaphragm, so this will take a lot of practice. Try taking a deep breath and watching your belly rise, and then when you are ready to let the air out, hiss and watch your belly fall. Do this ten times a day every day to get used to it, and then this will become second nature.

Now that we talked about breath, it's time to get in front of the mirror. I need you to do three things:

1. Part your lips into a smile. Not one that's stressed and forced but relaxed. Without moving your lips whatsoever, try to those ten diaphragm breaths.
2. Now try talking with your lips parted.
3. For fun, try saying the alphabet as you move your figure's lips.

Did that feel awkward? Yes! However, if it feels awkward it means you are doing it right. BRAVO! You just took another step towards becoming a professional ventriloquist.

You might be down on yourself about your rather visible and noticeable lip movement. Do not be discouraged. Most beginner vents struggle with these basics. That is why 30 minutes of practice daily is important.

Now let's talk about the alphabet. The letters B, F, M, P, and

V might have been especially difficult. (Note, for this book my puppet children wanted it to be known they do not struggle with these letters, it's "my people" who have the issues.)

Here are some things you can do to deal with those troublesome letters:

1. For B, say D. Instead of saying, "Bad boys," say "Dad doys." But think bad boys.
2. For F, say "eth". Instead of saying, "Phil is a funny fellow," say "ethil is a ethunny ethellow." But think "Phil is a funny fellow."
3. For m, say N. Instead of "Mary mashes mangos," say "Nary nashes nagos." But think "Mary mashes mangos."
4. For P say T. Instead of Peter is a Pilot, it's "Teter is a tilot." But think Peter is a pilot.
5. For W, say oy. Instead of "Why Wally," say "O-y o-aylly. Think Why Wally.

These adjustments will not only make the letters easier to say while maintaining both lip control and clarity, but the audience will not be any the wiser. While it seems a lot to digest now, over time as you continue to practice, this will become second nature.

Maybe you are substituting letters, but feel it is confusing and is frustrating you more, don't fret. There is a second way that helped me, and this is still my go-to when I have difficulty. Skip over the troublesome letters and go straight to the vowel. For instance:

1. Instead of saying "bad boys", say "ad oys." But think "bad boys."
2. Instead of saying "Phil is a funny fellow," say "il is a unny ellow." But think "Phil is a funny fellow."
3. Instead of "Mary mashes mangos" say "ary ashes angos." But think "Mary mashes mangos."
4. Instead of "Peter is a pilot," say "eter is an ilot." But think "Peter is a pilot."
5. Instead of "Why Wally," say "hy Ally." But think "Why Wally."

If a troublesome word continues to irk you, you can substitute an easier word until you master the troublesome word. For instance, instead of "bad boys," you could say, "evil guys." If your figure must say a troublesome word, as a ventriloquist you can repeat it. For instance, here is an example with one of my figures, Valley Girl May Wilson, featured on the cover of this book:

May Wilson: *Why do you like bad boys?*

April: *Wait, did you just ask me why I liked bad boys?*

That short cut not only helps keep the word from becoming completely lost, but keeps the routine moving. If the word is lost because the audience cannot understand your figure, not only is it sloppy ventriloquism, but there is nothing worse than someone saying, "I can't understand the puppet when it talks."

Another challenge for vents is plosive consonants, as in sounds that you use your lips to make, thus exploding at the front of the mouth and your lips moving quite a bit. (English has six plosive consonants: B, D, G, K, P and T.) These sounds are much harder to make if you are trying not to move your lips. Just like you did with hard words, skip over the plosives, go straight to the rest of the word, just like it was suggested in the second short cut above. For instance:

1. Instead of "Tinker Bell" say "Inker Ell." But think "Tinker Bell."
2. Instead of "Plosive" say "Losive." But think Plosive.
3. Instead of "Kinda" say "inda." But think Kinda
4. Instead of "Doghouse," say "Og House." But think Doghouse.

Now that you know the alphabet and how to say words that are harder, try to say some of the following complete sentences:

"Hello, how are you?"

"Hey, this totally rocks. Now who's the dummy?"

"You're putting words in my mouth."

After saying those sentences a few times, now it's time to say those sentences while you make your figure's mouth move. Not only are you perfecting the illusion that will make your act successful, but you are getting a basic knowledge of synch. In case you are wondering what I mean, synch is short for synchronizing. According to *Webster's Dictionary*, the definition of synchronizing is, "Occurring at the same time or rate."

Jim Henson stressed synch and I will do the same. I know it sounds like I am bogging you down with minutiae, but if you don't understand synch now, down the line it will be a problem. If your synch is off for any reason, the illusion is ruined. (I should also note there are some vents such as Taylor Mason who do a Kung Fu movie bit with bad dubbing, but this is not bad synch. This is very well rehearsed synch with a concept. There is a BIG DIFFERENCE.)

Another quick note about synch: Some newbie vents are so hyper-focused on lip control they neglect synch completely. While lip control is important, it is not the only component to ventriloquism. Good lip control + Bad Synch = Bad Ventriloquism. Think of it this way, every time you talk your mouth moves, right? Well, so does your figure's mouth.

From this point forward, as far as you are concerned, your figure is real. No, I don't mean in that scary movie kind of way, but the more you treat them like a real being, the more successful your act will be in front of an audience.

Do you move when you are talking and excited about something? Guess what: So does your figure! (They are real, remember?) For fun, every time your figure talks, try moving their arm, head or body in some way.

This not only adds to the essence and personality of your figure, but your figure isn't static nor is your figure suffering from dead hang.

Not only will your figure's movement make the act more exciting, but it will be a better way to get the audience engaged with their character. Additionally, the audience will also be less focused on your lip control, because as a ventriloquist they will be looking at your lips. A note about this, while movement is important, IT IS NO SUBSTITUTE FOR MASTERING THE VERY IMPORTANT CONCEPTS OF SYNC AND LIP CONTROL. (Yes Grasshopper, this is hard work.)

Now that you have worked on lip control, synch and movement, let's try giving that being on your arm a voice of their own. First, try saying the above sentences in a higher voice and muffle it, appearing as if the voice is coming from elsewhere. Then try saying those sentences in a lower voice, muffling it, as if the voice is coming from elsewhere. This is the beginning of what is known as "throwing your voice." Now try both again and see which you feel fits the figure on your arm.

If your voice is low, it will work better to give them a higher voice, and if your voice is high it is better to give them a lower voice. This will not only make the two voices distinctive, but add to the character and start to sculpt what is to become your act.

Now simply audio record the two of you talking. As an experiment, play the recording for a friend or family member and ask them who they think the second voice is. If they say it is you disguising your voice, go back to the mirror and keep practicing; if they think it's a new friend you have made, then you have been successful.

It is easy to get overwhelmed and feel that ventriloquism isn't for you, but don't give up. Becoming a good ventriloquist does not happen overnight. As a matter of fact, it takes years. I know it did in my case, and to this day I am proud to say I am still learning.

Take comfort in the fact that the community welcomes vents at all levels of experience and talent as long as they are serious about the art form. At ConVENTion, Mark Wade has had workshops on the schedule specifically geared towards beginner vents that deal with all the issues I have outlined above. If others see a newbie at ConVENTion struggling, the vent is not ostracized but embraced. Mark assures, "Don't worry, when their lips are moving we pull them aside and work with them."

Another note about lip control and technique, while it is part of being a ventriloquist, it is not all of being a ventriloquist. Character creation and writing a routine are also crucial, too. Steve Axtell has this piece of advice for young vents that I wish someone had told me once upon a time, "Nothing is worse than a ventriloquist trying to master lip control and they forgetting to have fun."

So regardless of where you are in the process, whether you are just beginning or are a seasoned professional, remember you are not training for combat or digging a ditch. You are talking to a puppet on your arm.

No, you do not have to learn ventriloquism. You get to learn ventriloquism, and this is a gift. I realize as a young vent you can become so serious and studious wanting to make a name for yourself and wanting very much to be good at what you do that you forget to enjoy the journey.

Ventriloquism, whether you are a major headliner, performing at a VFW hall, doing a small show for family and friends or are performing in front of your mirror, is just that, a journey.

In all of this the most important thing is to continue to HAVE FUN, because that will keep you learning and growing as a vent. Nothing is worse than viewing practice as a chore, because if you do that you will burn out. Venting that needs work and could be improved is better than no venting at all.

Now as you are on your journey and you are learning how to make the being on your arm talk, let's give your figure a personality. Want to know how to do that? Turn the page — after another April anecdote!

An April Anecdote

Setting: Cleveland Public Square, 2016 GOP National Convention.

Players: Donald J. Tramp (puppet), April (ventriloquist), Clinton Billups (April's manager), Cop (Cleveland PD), MAGAT (man in MAGA hat, handlebar mustache, open carry firearm), Stand Together Against Trump (STAT) protesters for whom Donald J. Tramp is spokespuppet.

Scene opens. April and Donald J. Tramp are performing their show in The Square when MAGAT approaches.

MAGAT: Why do you hate Donald Trump?

APRIL: I don't hate Trump…

MAGAT: Shut up. I was talking to him!

MAGAT points at Donald J. Tramp. Clinton signals to Cleveland PD Officer that there is a potentially dangerous situation.

MAGAT: Shut up little man! You need to stop disrespecting Trump! He is going to be our future leader!

Clinton and Cop see MAGAT is legit angry at a puppet and start laughing. STAT protestors muffle their giggles.

DONALD J. TRAMP: Fake news. I am Huuuuuuuge! Right baby?

Donald turns to April who nods. MAGAT, frustrated, stomps off.

Moral of the story: MAGAT wasn't stupid; puppets are real.

Donald J. Tramp TV Interview in Cleveland at 2016 GOP Convention

5 CREATING YOUR CHARACTER

In the last chapter, I mentioned treating your figures like they were real and made a joke about it not being in a scary movie kind of way. However, it is worth noting ventriloquists have been featured in countless plotlines in the horror film genre. This is because so many skilled vents have been that good at creating the semblance that the figures on their arms, aside from their ventriloquist, has a mind and personality all their own.

While purists in the vent community feel that such cinema has portrayed vent in a negative light, I could not disagree more. It adds to the lore around the art form, but it is also proof that the screenwriter in question saw a vent somewhere that gave them a memorable illusion and performance therefore being their muse. Additionally, it brings vent to a new audience and a viewer might be a little curious about learning the art form themselves. ("May Wilson here. April and I were in a scary movie called *Death of a Dummy*. Yes, it was fun. No, she was not acting.")

The point of my tale is that the more life you breathe into the character on your arm, the more the audience will treat them like they are real and forget they are a puppet. (However, both you and the audience know that it is still a puppet on your arm.) Additionally, not only will the audience like the character more, but your act will practically write itself.

You might argue that the figure on your arm is just a puppet built of household products, fabric, wood or latex. This is where I am going to stop you. That figure is a noun, which means it's a person, place, thing, animal, etc. Just like you, that figure has a backstory that has shaped their personality and the way they see the world.

Just like you exist with a first and last name, your character also needs a first and last name as part of their identity. You might argue a first name is sufficient. WRONG!

When I was getting my sea legs in NYC, I was blessed to work with the late great Otto Petersen of Otto and George at Pips Comedy Club. Otto headlined and May and I did a five minute guest spot between him and feature Chips Cooney. It was a decent set, but keep in mind I also was very green.

After the show, the comics all made the journey to El Greco's, a legendary diner in Sheepshead Bay, Brooklyn. We ate, drank, laughed and waxed poetic about comedy. Otto and George, legend has it, inspired the Corky and Fats characters in *Magic*. (A story Otto denied.) Otto Petersen was a vent I always admired. This meeting was a dream come true.

As we were kicking back after midnight on that hot July night in the outdoor dining area, Otto said, "April, I need to ask, what's May's last name?"

With a mouth full of food and pride I said, "She doesn't need a last name, she's a puppet."

Otto shook his head, "May has to have a last name. It will make her more real and have a good reason behind the last name."

Now I was curious, "What's George's last name?"

Otto said, "It's Dudley, George Dudley. Just like my uncle. Give it some thought."

For about a week my head spun. Calling her May Brucker would be odd and would make two of us with a last name that was hard to say. May Flowers just sounded corny.

Then it came to me one day as I was telling someone about growing up without cable and having only three channels. We began to discuss our favorite cartoons, one of mine at the time being *Dennis the Menace.* The friend I was talking to said, "What was the name of Dennis's neighbor?"

"Mr. Wilson," I said. Then it came to me, this was May's last name and thus May Wilson, the blonde gold digging puppet on my arm, was born. Not only did this connect, but it was certainly much easier to say than Brucker. ("May Wilson here again. My first and last name are the two hardest letters for a ventriloquist to say, making April the DUMMY.")

Not only does May have a last name, but so does any figure that comes into my collection for any reason. Now that your figure has a first and last name, it's time to get to know them.

Print these questions on a separate sheet of paper and write out the answers. Note, I got this inspiration from Paul Winchell once upon a time and these still help me:

1. Is your figure a person, animal, mineral, fruit, vegetable, plant, alien or other undeclared species?
2. What is your figure's gender identity and proper pronoun? Is your figure straight, LGBTQ identified or another species where these labels don't apply?
3. What is your figure's relationship status? Married, single, divorced, looking, etc.?
4. What is your figure's race/nationality? Are they even from Earth? (Note, I am not telling you what to do, but be mindful not to make your character an insulting trope if you are making a figure that is of a race different than yours.)
5. Where was your figure born and in what year?
6. What was your figure's childhood/home life like?
7. Is your figure educated or uneducated?
8. Is your figure religious, spiritual, atheistic? And do they believe in an afterlife?
9. What is your figure's occupation?
10. How did you meet your figure?
11. What is your relationship to your figure?

12. What is your figure most passionate about?
13. What are your figure's pet peeves?
14. Does your figure have any fears?
15. What is your figure's biggest dream in life?
16. If your figure were to have dinner with one person, who would it be?
17. Who does your figure love most?
18. Who does your figure loathe most?
19. If you were to leave the room right now, what would your figure say about you?
20. If your figure were to go to a film or a concert, what would they see?
21. Has your figure ever travelled or have they never left their hometown?
22. Does your figure have children?
23. What is your figure's motivation?
24. What is your figure most ashamed of?
25. If your figure had a bedroom, what would it look like?
26. What does your figure eat for breakfast?
27. Is your figure a bath or shower person and how do they like the water temperature?
28. Is your figure outgoing or shy?
29. Is your figure liberal or conservative in their political beliefs?
30. If you asked your figure to fill out this list about you, what would they say?

As I was writing this book, I spoke with Nigel Dunkley. We both admitted the Paul Winchell's questions have helped us in the past and still continue to steer us in the right direction.

For Nigel, these questions helped form the Cindy Hot Chocolate's character as a rapper, but helped him find his character as Cindy's mentor/manager. Nigel and Cindy not only have gone viral, but have been featured on *The Steve Harvey Show*.

These questions can also serve down the line when you are experiencing writer's block. Not only will these take you back to the basics of your relationship, but can help you think of new material you never even dreamed of. (More about writing later.)

An aside about your relationship to your figure, think long and hard about this one. Not only will this be the basis for your act, but it will be another source of material. A lot of comedy is conflict, so in deciding what your relationship is with your figure, where is the conflict? For May Wilson and me, she is the obnoxious roommate who is always looking for a sugar daddy and all I want to do is find Mr. Okay and live peacefully. Unfortunately, I cannot kick May out because I am too broke to live on my own and need the help with the expenses. ("May Wilson here again. April really can't kick me out because she needs me for the act.")

Next, in the creation of your figure, in order to get to know them better I am going to challenge you to give them a personal object. You might want to know what is a personal object and what does this have to do with my ventriloquism?

A personal object, if you have ever had an acting class, specifically "The Method," is something someone carries with them of some importance. Many actors will bring a personal object to set that helps them channel the role/experience that they are trying to create. Giving your character a personal object might help make their experience and existence more authentic.

You yourself might unknowingly have a personal object that you look at in times of distress for comfort such as a ribbon from a spelling bee, an old family photo, a lucky stone, a rabbit's foot, etc. If your figure had a similar thing, what would it be?

Might it be a picture of a significant other, a lucky pair of sunglasses, a poem by Robert Frost, a NASCAR ticket stub or a rock from their home planet? For my figure, May Wilson, it is a photo of Anna Nicole Smith, her hero, and she glances at it when she needs inspiration to keep going on her search for a sugar daddy and reality show fame.

What does this have to do with forming an act? Consider this more savings in your ventriloquist bank account. You might not need it now, but when you need it, you will have it. The more you put in, the more you will be able to take out in case of a writer's block related emergency.

My next question to you is, if your figure was alone and didn't know they were being watched, what would they do? Again, if you have ever taken an acting class this is what is known as Private Moment. No, I don't mean anything seedy or dirty. Who is your figure in secret when no one is watching?

For instance, if your character is shy, do they start dancing to hip hop music? If your character is more outgoing and louder, do they sit and journal about life? If your character is a stereotypical NASCAR fan, are they reading Shakespeare? If your character is more professorial, are they cheering loudly at *BattleBots?* May Wilson, who was born poor in Pocatello, ID, looks at the photo of herself in front of her trailer home when she was nothing more than a dirty sock. (May is rather defensive about her past and once told me the term was, "financially challenged." Please don't tell her I told you any of this.)

As of this moment, the two of you are a comedy duo. One of you will be the so called "straight man" and the other the "comedic foil." The two of you have to be different because again, the conflict is in the comedy. So, as you construct their personality, do the same exercises on yourself. The better you know your figure and the better you know yourself, the better your act will be.

For instance, when you set a table you don't have two pepper shakers or two saltshakers. You have a salt and pepper shaker. To have two of the same not only does not make sense, but there is no act any other way.

Before I give you your homework assignment, let's talk about accents. Don't give your figure an accent unless it really makes sense with their character. An accent will get an easy laugh, but it is also lazy comedy if there is no character or work behind it. So, if you are giving your character an accent, ask yourself if it makes sense for the character and if you are leaning on it solely for a gag? If it makes sense and it's not a gag, use it. Even with an accent regardless of where it originates, if you do the work, your figure is still very real with three dimensions.

A second note about accents in regard to race and culture: If you are not a member of a marginalized group, be careful about creating a character who is. I am not telling you how to do your act, but be aware that this can be taken the wrong way. Remember, your job as a ventriloquist is to entertain, not to purely insult. There is a line between being funny and being a bully. I am not trying to censor you, but don't be a bully. It's bad comedy, lacks creativity and is lazy ventriloquism.

If you have any questions about your character choice and you choose to go this route, show it to a member of the group your figure is from. In the event they think it's funny, go ahead and test the waters. (In my experience, this feedback has even given me some suggestions on how to make the character better and the act funnier.) If not, go back to the drawing board and check your motives for creating the character. While I do not want to censor you, I do want you to be the best ventriloquist you can be.

Now, before going to the next chapter, I am going to give you some homework. Watch some Abbot and Costello, Laurel and Hardy or, if you want to go more modern, Key and Peel. Why? Because this is how you should see yourself and your figure and it will help you when it comes to writing your act.

Great writing is the key to great Vent routines!
ANTIOCH UNIVERSITY
LOS ANGELES

6 WRITING A ROUTINE

You have learned the basics of ventriloquism and created a character, now it is time to write a routine for this new comedy duo you created.

Write as much as you can and whenever you have an idea that inspires you, jot it down whether it is in a notebook, your computer or on your phone. This will help you create things that will excite and inspire you.

You might ask, what if you are moved to write a short story, something that could be a masterpiece but not necessarily have anything to do with your act. I say write the story because it is all interconnected. Writing in any medium is good. This means you are not only observing the world around you, but are generating ideas and this will eventually come in handy for your act.

Heck, you might get so inspired as you get to know your figure and yourself that you write solo standup material for you. This is only good, because the more you know yourself, the more you can know your figure and the better you two can be together.

Additionally, if you are hoping to make a career in showbiz, developing as a legit standup can only help you as some club owners and bookers will not book "prop acts," a group that vents are lumped into. (I do both legit standup and vent in my longer sets.) This increases your number of bookings, will make you have even more fun writing jokes and will make you even more confident when it comes to comedy.

Remember, even as you get comfortable in your own comedy skin, when your partner comes out you two are still a duo. Steve Hewlett, finalist on *Britain's Got Talent*, gives this writing advice to vents, "Write all the time. I write for myself as well as my puppet. But remember, always let your puppet be the funny one."

Now that we are on the subject of writing and you, let's talk about material. Many vents feel that just because they have a puppet on their arm they don't have to talk about themselves let alone talk at all and can fade in the background. I was guilty of this as a young vent, partially because I was quite shy and suffered from stage fright.

However, a comedy comrade gave me the best piece of advice, "We see May and that's great, but we don't see you. And if we don't see you, the audience can't root for you when May insults you. You have figured out who May is and once you figure out who you are, the jokes will come."

My friend was right. Not only did me speaking more make

the act better, but the audience got a sense of who I was and therefore it made May's jokes and insults funnier. (This was the one time May was okay with me speaking more.)

So, when you think about material, realize that offstage you are a complete person, too. This life offstage is a gold mine for material whether you are a student, teacher, parent, sibling, aunt, uncle, coworker, neighbor and the list goes on. If executed properly, this can be a treasure trove of things for your figure to roast you about. (Yes, puppets are judgmental rascals, but the audience loves it.)

Now a note about real life material: This is a hot debate in the comedy world. Some people are nervous about sharing about their lives because they don't want to be identified offstage for a number of reasons. It is okay to change names and some facts; it is an act after all.

Then some people make things up entirely because it is an "act" and you will be doing this to some extent because your partner does not file taxes or have a social security number. Some people will discourage you from doing this and treat the suggestion like it is blasphemy. The great fiction writer and teacher Percival Everett once said, "When it comes to writing fiction, do not be handcuffed by the truth."

Writing a vent routine is writing fiction in some ways as your partner is a puppet, so if a joke is funny and it's not "real," don't be afraid to use it. Also, if you exaggerate something and it gets a laugh, keep it. The key to comedy, just like ventriloquism is misdirection. So, if it works and you hear laughter, the bit is doing its job.

That being said, if you want to get completely personal and "real," do it. Not only will you be connected to the material, but your act will be harder to steal. (Yes, there are joke thieves.) I find some of my best material is true to life.

This is when I have to issue a warning, while going for pathos is good, avoid making your act a therapy session with you and your puppet. Working out your issues will make you a complete person and heal wounds, but an audience is not paying to see that. I have seen comedians use the comedy stage as a substitute for much needed therapy and it always elicits awkward silence from the audience.

Seinfeld said it best on an episode of *Comedians in Cars Getting Coffee* when discussing the comedians of today with Dana Carvey, "I am 58 and I have responsibilities. When I go to a comedy club, I don't want pathos, I want to laugh." So, if you are going to get "real," keep the punchlines at the end."

The second place your material will come from is your relationship to your partner. This is why you did all that work in the previous chapter and this is why I asked you to find conflict, because a lot of your material will also come from that conflict in that relationship.

So, what is your conflict? Are you a biker dude and is she a church lady lecturing you about how to live? Are you a corporate lady type and is he a rowdy biker dude, always keeping you up with his parties? Are you an okay student, and are they the overachiever always asking for extra homework? Are you the teacher and is he the most troublesome kid in the class?

For May Wilson and me, we are forced to be roommates because we are two broke single gals. To make matters worse, May is the worst roommate ever, but I can't kick her out. So, if that's not conflict, I don't know what is.

The same goes if your figure is non-human. If your figure is a sock, is he/she/they sick and tired of being on your dirty foot and feel the need to tell everyone? If your figure is a plant or a dog, does he/she/they witness the world around you and have a lot of opinions, especially about your life? If your figure is an alien, how do they feel about Earthlings, and how do they respond to your life as an Earthling?

A word about delivery, good comedy and good delivery are honest and not forced. When performing your routine with your figure, do not try too hard to chase the laugh or sling punchlines. Doing this will not only make you feel tired, but your audience will not laugh because your delivery will be stilted.

Instead of going for the laugh, have a conversation with your figure and go for the truth. In going for the truth, you will always get the laugh. Comedy always comes from the truth of any situation and the more sincere you aim to be the more successful your act will be.

The best comedy in real life is when people or beings are not trying to be funny, but instead are being their authentic selves whether it is a dog trying to eat a fly, a teenager lying to get out of a math test, parents having awkward conversations with their kids, grandparents getting excited about bingo, your super sports fan family member after the win/loss of his favorite team and the list goes on.

I know many of you reading this book want to be the greatest ventriloquist who ever lived. You want to be adored by all of your fans. (I hope you are, because then you can say my book taught you everything you know and I can sell more copies.) In that daydream, I know you want to see your name in lights and you will be the coolest cat who ever walked the puppet stage. You might be, but don't be that cool cat onstage.

Why? BECAUSE COOL IS THE ENEMY OF COMEDY. Own your flaws and your ineptitude, because it is not only part of the fabric that makes you who you are, but it's gonna be darn good comedy and will bring you a lot of laughs.

What are your flaws? Have people teased you about your ears, your eyes or the way you talk? (I have a very noticeable Pittsburgh accent that my audience can so hear, and boy do my puppets have fun with me.) Are you bad at math, a terrible driver, always late, always sleep, etc.? Now this gives you more material for your act, and more things for your puppet to roast you about. (I cannot tell you how many digs my children take at me. Ungrateful snots.)

In talking about honesty and not being cool, yes it is okay to honor and acknowledge the fact your partner is a puppet. I know, I told you they are real, but they are also a puppet. As

I said before and let me say it again, the audience knows they are a puppet, you know they are a puppet, and they know they are a puppet. It's okay to put it in the act because it makes it even funnier when your partner gives it right back to you. This is helping to employ irony which according to *Webster's Dictionary* means, "The expression of one's meaning by using language that normally signifies the opposite, typical for humorous or emphatic effect."

Irony comes from the truth of the situation, so the more you try to own yourself and your partner, the more successful you will be.

I say this over and over again in this book, but when you perform HAVE FUN. The more fun you are having, the more fun they will have and the laughs will come all the more easily.

Before we get to joke writing formula, I feel it's important to talk about punching up and punching down. This is very important in comedy and separates an amateur from a pro.

Punching up means making fun of yourself or making fun of people at a higher socio-economic station. Many of the great vent acts and comedians punch up. Not only is it funny because it puts you in a place of vulnerability, but it also takes true talent and you could really make some great commentary. Punching up is funnier because it makes the material more universal and identifiable for your audience.

Punching down means making fun of someone at a lower station than you in life, whether it's socioeconomic or otherwise. Yes, punching down will get you the easier laugh, but you want to avoid doing it if you can. One, there is a big difference between being a great ventriloquist and a bully. Second, punching down is lazy joke writing and will not get the big laughs that punching up will.

You might cite the example of Bubba J and Jeff Dunham, as Bubba is often drunk and slow, same with Mortimer Snerd and Knucklehead Smiff characters before him. However, these are stock characters who appear dim witted, but often outsmart their ventriloquist. So that is not punching down, that is very clever punching up where the puppet gets the upper hand.

Another example that many vents who are more into standup comedy might cite is Otto Peterson and his partner George Dudley, whom I spoke about in a previous chapter. Yes, George was insulting, but he was insulting to everyone. (He was once termed Don Rickles in a puppet's body.) The work on George's character was not only very good, but he made sure to punched in every direction making sure everyone got hit.

A quick note about insult comedy, I am a fan of Don Rickles, Triumph, as well as Otto and George, but play at your own risk. If this is who you feel your character is, try it out. If not, don't worry about it, there is no harm in experimenting. However, if you choose to go this route you have to be VERY FUNNY.

Now to the mechanics of writing a vent act. Be aware that

when you write your act, you are not simply writing jokes and a punchline, but a script. This is why I had you do the homework in the last chapter. It is not simply the jokes that make the act funny, but the situation and the relationship between two characters.

Let's talk about how to write a joke. There must be a set-up and a punchline. The set-up is the beginning of the joke, the punchline is the pay off. Let me show you with an oldie but goodie:

Set Up = *Why did the chicken cross the road?*

Punchline = *To get to the other side.*

What makes the punchline of that joke work? You don't see it coming and much like a magic trick, it's a misdirection with a miraculous result. (Okay, maybe not that joke, but it proves my point.)

Writing punchlines is where your talent and creativity will come in. The late great Mitch Hedberg gave this piece of writing advice to a headliner I worked with and he passed it on to me, "Don't go with the first punchline that pops into your head. Go with the third."

Now let's talk about your vent routine. Take everything I have given you and write your first script for you and your partner. If you need a reference, here is a sample vent routine I wrote for a teacher and her figure, Woody Woodmere. The teacher is very stern, and Woody, a wooden figure, is the worst behaved child in class:

Teacher: *Woody, do your work.*

Woody: *Teach, I'm like you. I take my summers off.*

Teacher: *Woody, it's not summer. It's winter.*

Woody: *Not true. Right now, it is summer in South America.*

Teacher: *Well right now it's study hall time which means quiet.. I guess you weren't listening.*

Woody: *Your lesson today taught us it was summer in South America. Guess you weren't listening.*

Teacher: *Young man with that attitude you will never have a job.*

Woody: *Teach, it's cause I'm on the same plan you are.*

Teacher: *Which is….*

Woody: *Retirement.*

Teacher: *That's not true. I'm still working.*

Woody: *Exactly. But you're old enough to be retired. See, I should be teaching.*

Teacher: *Then go to college and become teacher.*

Woody: *Wait, you need a college degree to do this?*

Teacher: *That's it. Enough of this tomfoolery.*

Woody: *Suspension means vacation. Yippee!*

Teacher: *Nope. I have a real punishment.*

Woody: *Listen to you teach some more?*

Teacher: *No, the pencil sharpener!*

Woody: *Not the pencil sharpener....NOOOOOO!!!! I PROMISE I'LL BE GOOD!*

(Woody starts crying.)

Teacher: *Alright, you are a good kid sometimes. Do your work and let me check on the rest of the class.*

(Teacher turns back. Has a sign that says KICK ME. Woody laughs and whispers.)

Woody: *Gotchya!*

Teacher: *What?*

Woody: *Nuthin, teach.*

The above is a sample script with set ups and punchlines throughout, establishing both characters and their reality. You can use this script if you want, but I encourage you to use this as a basis to write your own because my scripts and characters cannot do your ideas justice.

If you do not feel ready to write your own routine and need other references, AxTrax from Axtell Expressions also sells pre-written scripts for vents. Again, I encourage you to write your own material, but the more scripts you read and the more vent acts you watch, the better idea you will have on how to write for you and your partner.

You might also write and be afraid of bringing your routine out in public because it does not work. Newsflash: Bombing is a part of the process. Even as a pro, you will lay an egg every once in a while. If someone denies bombing, either they aren't doing enough shows or they are lying. (May Wilson says she never bombs, but insists that I have bombed plenty of times.)

Bombing might hurt your ego, but it is a chance to go back to the drawing board. Sometimes the jokes you wrote need different punchlines or you need to strengthen your delivery. In the case of Taylor Mason, your character needs tweaking in order for it to work.

As he once told me, Taylor performed for an agent showcase with Sumo, one of his most well-known puppets. Before that, he had struggled with Sumo and was thinking of taking him out of the act. That is, until a young woman who was acting as an assistant to an agent saw the act. While she did not have a strong background in show business, she had an idea: Audience participation should be a part of Sumo's schtick.

Taylor decided to give her suggestion a shot and suddenly Sumo was a hit. Not only did this change make all the difference, but Sumo is now one of Taylor's best known figures and one of the most successful parts of his show today. (As an aside, I first came across Taylor Mason when I was a little vent and Sumo was my favorite of all of his characters.)

Perform whenever possible, whether it is family, friends, roommates or people who you trust that can give you feedback. Not only will you get an outside view of your act, but it will make you stronger.

However, be weary, there is some feedback you shouldn't take. After a show, a girlfriend of mine suggested May Wilson argue with a Salvador Dali puppet onstage. In the case of feedback like this, you smile, thank them and put it in your mental trash bin. Over time, you will be able to sort the good from the bad.

There are a lot of growing pains involved in being a ventriloquist. While I encourage you to resist the temptation of quitting, I also want you to resist the temptation of resting on your laurels after victory. There is always a new level to reach, always more to achieve. I am still growing as a ventriloquist and so are the puppets I perform with. I wish the same for you and your partner(s).

My one-woman stage show in Las Vegas

7 VENTRILOQUISM AS A CAREER

In the famous Disney cartoon, Pinocchio, the marionette who longs to be a real human boy, sings a diddly, "Hi-Diddle-Dee-Dee, an actor's life for me." Although this puppet wasn't cool enough to be a vent figure, he gave us a tune which showbiz people have all quoted at least once in their lives. (The tune was written by Walter Catlett and if you want to do this showbiz thing for real, you've got to credit everyone involved.)

The lyrics of the song illustrate the showbiz fantasy perfectly. There is this romantic notion of life on the road where you get to see the world from New York to Vegas to Hollywood, and every major city in between. You see your name in bright lights, flashing against the city night as throngs of people are lined up around the block to see your show. As you live out of your suitcase touring the world, you see the different captions you post on social media as you and your puppet stand in front of the Eiffel Tower because why not?

Your family thinks and probably also tells you that you've lost your mind when you say to them, poised with your Groucho Marx figure, "I'm going to make a career out of this." (Okay, maybe just me.)

Your friends smile and nod thinking it's cool you have ambitions outside of your small town or office cubicle. Secretly, behind your back, they either say you don't really have the goods (friends is a broad term) or indulge your flight of fancy believing that you will land on Earth and resume the need to lead a conventional life. Pshaw on that, you will show them all! (The most fun part is always you showing them and your friends being impressed that you actually followed through.)

At night when no one is watching, your dreams are filled with ventriloquism superstardom. During the day you scour the Internet watching videos of your favorite vents and even discovering a few new vents. When said new favorites accept your social media friend requests, you feel your life is one step closer to being complete. You read the bios of famous ventriloquists and how-to books on vent hoping to gain insight, inspiration and knowledge. Watching your clock, you are counting the minutes to the day when you will take your suitcase, hit the road and show everyone what you and your puppet partner have got.

While dreams are important and are the first step in creating art that could change the world, let me give you a dose of reality. You have picked one of the most difficult artistic careers in the world. I don't say this to discourage you because you could very well be the next great vent and the community has a lot of wonderful talent coming up. (Yourself included.) I am proud of you for wanting this, but it would also be cruel if I did not warn you about what you are about to face.

If you decide to embark on this career path, financial insecurity will be a reality. This won't be because you will fail, but due to the uncertainty of the tide of the business. There will be seasons you will work a lot and have no time for anything outside of gigging and seasons that you will not work at all and be scrambling to keep a roof over your head. Even the big stars deal with this feast or famine reality. (As an aside, The Actors' Fund and Comedy Gives Back are wonderful resources that do financial wellness workshops for performers addressing cash flow issues.)

Due to the nature of this beast, you will be forced to be married to your career which means you run the risk of not only your relationships suffering, but being outright nonexistent. Many vents travel frequently for work, which makes having a personal life of any sort very difficult. When not working, it is nearly impossible to have a "normal" life of any sort, as you are always chasing work, auditioning, sending out press packets or waiting by the phone.

There is an old adage about the theatre, "Many are called but few are chosen." So, if you can see yourself doing anything else, do it. The world needs creative and talented people everywhere, not just show business.

However, if you are dead set on doing this and doggedly determined, welcome aboard. I am here to offer my support and guidance. Are you still crazy enough to want to do this for real? Let me talk about how to get to your vent dreams, some of what you will face and how to deal with it.

If you are an independent adult doing vent, sick of the office job wanting to escape Dunder Mifflin, do not quit your day job. Why? Because at the beginning you will be doing many gigs for low or no pay and you will still need a roof over your head. Headshots, a website and professional figures cost money. While you might hate your job, unless you become a SAG-AFTRA or Equity member who works regularly, you will be uninsured.

This might not sound like a big deal to younger readers, but a health emergency can cost a pretty penny. This doesn't necessarily have to include a fatal illness or a broken bone, but also basic dental care, which is very expensive out of pocket. If you are working a support job that you dislike, look at it not as a grind, but as the thing to finance your ultimate goal of becoming a professional ventriloquist.

If you are a student vent, do not drop out of school. Maybe you are gaining some traction in student talent shows and you want to take the act on the road. That's fine, but finish college. As a talent agent told me when I was 20 years old, "A degree not only looks good, but industry people like an education. It means you work hard, have goals and can talk about things other than ventriloquism. And you might get sick of this one day and work might dry up. You might be hot today, but might not be hot tomorrow."

That agent was correct. Everyone's phone stops ringing for a variety of reasons. Humans grow and change, but so do their dreams. Regardless of whatever life throws at you, that college degree will be in your possession and no one can take that away. There are indeed some stars who have dropped out of college and hit the big time, but these are the exception and not the rule.

During my time at NYU, I had several classmates who left school because they felt that fame was just around the corner. Unfortunately, this was not the case. Most were not ready emotionally, mentally or skill wise for the demands they were facing professionally and personally. Running back to the fold of college, they were fighting for their spots in their perspective programs and sometimes they were gone. The other issue was financial aid and while they were able to secure it previously, they could not once they returned to school because they interrupted their education. In the end, jumping ship too early was not worth it. (Jay Johnson performed summers at Six Flags during college graduating on time, while Jeff Dunham took semesters off to tour but still finished.)

As a young vent college is a great safe place to be. You can learn life lessons in a controlled environment, not in a professional setting. Campus open mics and college variety nights are great places to cut your teeth, but you can also create a ready-made fan base. You also can take an improv class or join an improv or sketch comedy team. While it's not vent, it is a way for you to relax, hone your comedy chops, get an education and make your parents happy — a win-win.

Additionally, there also is a large market for college performers. There are many college and variety competitions that not only are catered towards college-aged comedians, but welcome ventriloquists. It's a great way to not only network, but also to meet performers your age. These people will not only love chasing the spotlight as much as you do, but could become lifelong friends.

Offstage, inside the classroom, whatever you major in can also help strengthen your performance tool kit. At NYU, I was an acting major and my degree has made me confident onstage. During college, I did workshops with casting directors and several of my classmates who moved into the production side of things still call me for auditions, especially when they need a comedian, ventriloquist or puppeteer.

Academically, I took several writing classes, which led to me getting stronger at putting words on the page. A playwriting elective not only made me realize I was good at writing comedy plays, but helped me bring that skill set to the routines I created with my puppets. Additionally, this led to me pursuing a parallel career as a writer, ultimately receiving an MFA in both Creative Nonfiction and Screenwriting from Antioch University Los Angeles. These degrees have given me the tools to craft one-person plays and television specials with my puppets, but also have helped me pen the text you are reading now. Someday I hope to teach classes at the college level to young performers who want to write and create their own work. Yes, my puppets will be helping. The only reason any of this is possible is because I stayed in school.

Even if your degrees are not performance or creative based, they can still help with your vent career. Mark Wade's teaching degree gave him the tools to become the nation's number one kid's vent, not only because he understands how his young audience thinks, but also the teachers and administrators since he was once one of them. Jay Johnson's business degree helped him off-screen, as it gave him the tools to not only negotiate his early contracts, but to get a copyright on *Soap* costar Bob Campbell so that he could use him in live performances. Bottom line, no educational opportunity is ever wasted.

As you embark on this journey, if you are sure your goal is to go "full time" at some point, make a list of what you want and what you need. If you want to be the world's greatest ventriloquist and are willing to sacrifice everything for vent, great. If you want a family, a house and security, then ask yourself if it is worth sacrificing some of those creature comforts to pursue your passion.

If the answer is yes and you want to sacrifice everything for vent, great. I myself have given up quite a bit and I feel it has been worth it. However, even as I have acquired an "impressive" list of credits, I have friends who did not feel the sacrifices were worth it and have enjoyed a career on a smaller scale that included the ability to have an almost normal life.

You might ask, "Who's more successful?" The answer is, it's a tie, because we are not only doing what makes us happy, but we are living our best and most complete lives. Now you might want to know what I think you should do. I can't answer that question, only you can. Just know the vent community needs vents at all levels, because it's not only good for morale, but also for the longevity of the art form.

Now if you are a woman hoping to make this a career, I need to get real with you because I don't want you to be rudely surprised about what is lurking ahead. You have two strikes against you in show business: One, you are a woman and people will not think you are funny because of your gender; Two, you are a prop act.

Prop acts are regarded as "hacks" in some comedy circles, and there are bookers and club owners who will not book ventriloquists, let alone women. They will not be shy about telling you either. Some regular standup comics will look down on you because they feel you cheat by using a prop to get a laugh. You also will have to work much harder than your male counterparts at any given time to prove yourself to both industry and audience alike and having a puppet on your arm only adds to that workload.

The good news is that you can rise above all of this by being the best ventriloquist and comic you can be. Sure, maybe some regular standup comics might not respect you at first, but once they see you have a well-written and funny act and that you are a good ventriloquist, you will earn their admiration and will have new fans in your corner. Additionally, club owners and bookers like funny acts that audiences enjoy and, if you fit this category, work will flow your way. There will always be people who won't book you and there will always be people who will for a variety of different reasons. If they don't want you, it's their loss.

Have a good support network. The benefit of this chosen family is that they listen when you are frustrated, but will be a suggestion sounding board when you need to advocate for yourself in any way, shape or form. This support network can include other vents, performer friends, understanding normie friends or family, and of course an agent or manager. They can help you navigate the uncertain waters of showbiz while you keep your positive attitude.

If you are someone with a family, this also may work against you. Many bookers are weary of booking acts with spouses and children since, in their experience, people with overhead may flake out because of a spouse who gets resentful that their partner is traveling so much. Then the booker must scramble to find a replacement act — a feat which is much harder than people think. Many club owners, bookers, agents and other industry folks have family themselves and understand the importance yours has to you, but they also have a business to run and a venue to fill. If this does not happen, their children might not eat or have new school clothes. Just as you have responsibilities so do they, remember that.

An added strike is if you are a woman with a family. Club owners fear female performers with children will be an extra liability because, in their experience, they have been hours late to performances or missed a club date when their kids have gotten sick. There also have been instances where a female performer has bailed on a club date at the insistence of a jealous boyfriend/husband. Most club owners are men who are weary of booking female talent to begin with and added with experiences like this from the past, they will pass on a female act even if she is funny.

Then there have been instances where well-intended female performers, wanting to honor a club date, but having a sitter bail for a myriad of reasons, bought their children to the gig. While many staffers and venue owners are parents themselves, the presence of a young child unfortunately could mean losing a liquor license. Life happens and people are often sympathetic, but it also puts staff and room operators in an awkward position. As a result, the door not only closes for said performer, but for other female acts as well.

I am saying to prioritize family; it's important. Yes, you can refuse a gig if you want to spend time with your family, but don't accept a gig and flake out because you can't balance your personal life.

That being said, you can still have a family life and your vent career, but continual dialogue with your partner and your support network are crucial. That way you can have your partner watch the kids if you have a club date. If you are a single parent, you can have a friend/family member help as you learn to adjust to your strange hours. (If this is the case, please leave your child with someone you know well. No club date or amount of money is worth the safety of your child.) Just make sure they are reliable and have more than one go-to person because sitters do back out for a variety of reasons. Your dreams don't have to be scaled down because you have a family life, but just like being a working parent in any other profession, this career does and will have its drawbacks.

Steve Hewlett of *Britain's Got Talent* said, "I don't take any contract that takes me away from my family. I read bios of famous vents and comedians who missed their kids growing up and I don't want to be that dad."

When he does have to be away from his family, Steve has added a provision in his contracts that his wife and children join him for a stretch of time and the Hewlett's take a family selfie commemorating their part in all of their father's VENTastic voyages.

If you choose to go this route, this can be a great way not only to have family time, but also to have an amazing family vacation. However, make sure your partner understands that you are working. As a performer, you have an agent/manager/booker you have to answer to and your partner is not welcome to make unnecessary demands upon your employers for any reason. You need to make this clear with your partner before you even pack your bags.

Minor children should be not only be tended to at all times, but make sure they understand they must be on their best behavior. ("We can have fun, but Mommy/Daddy is working.") Venue staff are not babysitters, and is not their job to discipline your children. While many club owners have families of their own, yours are not their responsibility and to assume otherwise makes you unaware and entitled. Not only does this create an unpleasant working environment for all, but it could lead to you getting fired. I know this sounds like common sense, but a great many entertainers have burned bridges and set their careers back because they could not establish proper boundaries between their personal and professional lives.

That being said, there also will be industry people who are understanding when it comes to the challenges of having a career onstage and a family in real time. In my experience, I have seen club owners who are not only sensitive to comedian mothers who are breast feeding, but actually tell them they can pump if need be. I have also seen "mom comics" and "mom vents" take other performers who have young children under their wing and give them helpful tips on how to achieve the onstage/offstage balance working moms in show biz strive to have. Yes, there are understanding people. You just need to know where to find them.

For female vents, and mom vents especially, there is a Facebook group called "The Ladies of Ventriloquism." In this online forum, not only is this a place to network with other female vents, but it is a safe place to talk about the challenges of being a woman in the industry. Additionally, it is also a place for Moms who are pursuing vent to get advice on the art/life balance that comes with being a professional ventriloquist. Not only are the Moms in the group helpful, but they have encountered many of the challenges I listed above of being a female act and then some.

Outside of the church and family show market, there is also a whole new market emerging for mothers who are performers. Mom Comedy Shows are not only popping up around the country, but searching for variety acts and a mom ventriloquist would be more than welcome. Just like your college comrades, not only is this a chance to network, but also to create a community.

In some of these shows, which are mostly earlier and where there is no alcohol served, children are welcome so the whole family can come. If you do it right, not only can your kids be a part of your journey and give you a lot of material, but they might go on to become your biggest fans not only onstage, but in real time too. You will show them not only that their dreams do matter, but that you can go after them at any stage in life.

If you embark on this career and discover it's not for you, it's not a detriment against you as a person. This occupation and the lifestyle that comes with it are not suitable for everyone. While it's tragic because many of my colleagues who have jumped ship were truly talented, tenacity is also a big part of the recipe for success in this business. Just as talent cannot be taught, neither can that.

If you need to step away from vent for any reason, whether it's family, personal or just because you need a sanity break, do it. Your happiness is crucial, and if you are falling apart you cannot do your best work, let alone be your best self. Put you first. Whether it's a week, a month, a year, many years, vent will still be there if and when you choose to come back to it.

If you step away and don't come back, then maybe you did what you were supposed to do with vent and that's fine. Everyone's journey is different, and you will be a better person for pursuing your dreams. As famed advertising executive Leo Burnett once said, "When you reach for the stars, you may not quite get one, but you won't get a handful of mud either."

If you step away and it pulls you back in, this is because you are supposed to doing vent. Let me tell you a secret, in the event it does pull you back in, it's because it is truly your calling and it will not let you quit. In the two times the business kicked my butt so hard, I wanted to throw in the towel; vent not only reeled me back in, but made me love it even more.

Vent might also open the door to a whole new love. Many young performers discover that while they are passionate about being onstage, their true calling is behind the scenes. This can lead to a career path as an entertainment lawyer, club owner, talent agent, personal manager, director, producer, etc. If this ends up being your destiny, not only will you be vitally important to young vents because you can employ them, but you can also add the expertise of having been on their side of things once upon a time.

If you become a working vent and are getting enough gigs and decide to go "full time," quitting the day job, eyeing your truck and singing the tune Pinocchio made ever so popular, Mark Wade offers a piece of advice that I wish I got once upon a time: "Save six months' salary for lean times. You will need the cushion."

If you are a vent who has a family that has decided to go full time, have an honest talk with your partner about finances. In addition to the stress of always having a partner who's away on the road, financial insecurity might be another issue. This is why it is important to be honest and open about the family budget from the beginning. Money, in addition to the other factors that make up a show biz career, are the number one reason for divorce. While a breakup of a relationship because you need to follow your dreams might happen, try to make sure your side of the street is clean, especially if there are minor children involved.

If you have to do this for real and you lose a partner because they don't understand your need to follow your dreams, this unfortunately goes with the territory. However, it has a silver lining. For me it was a *Daily Mail* article that went viral long before COVID-19 made it cool.

Even if you become the world's great vent, there is still

always more work to be done and more to achieve. A true pro never feels completely happy and they always know they can improve; this is why continually writing, practicing and honing your craft are vitally important. Even at the highest level with tremendous TV credits, a ventriloquist still must be good. The late Bob Vincent, talent agent and booker for Harrah's, said it best, "Every time you step onstage for an audience, you audition for them. An audience will pay to see you once and if you are not good, they will not pay to see you again."

If you are dead set, bound and determined to do this, even when things are at their darkest, you will find a way to make this work and it will be a life beyond your wildest dreams. Sure, there have been times where I wasn't sure how I was going to eat or pay my rent, but there is nothing like stepping onstage and pulling May Wilson out and having people fall in love with her.

May Wilson is the greatest performer of all time and men want her and women want to be her. Did I mention she is looking for a sugar daddy? Are you a sugar daddy?

Okay, it appears May Wilson has hijacked my manuscript. This is another occupational hazard of being a professional vent.

You still want to be the greatest ventriloquist ever; let's talk about what you will need to market yourself… right after another April anecdote.

An April Anecdote

When I graduated from NYU, I had my BFA in Theatre, my dreams and my puppets, but no job to pay the bills. After interviewing at a bunch of corporate offices and crying, I watched the movie *Beaches*. Getting inspired by Bette Midler in her bunny suit, I landed a job as a singing telegramer.

One crisp, winter day I was hired to deliver a Wonder Woman singing telegram to Marishka Hargitay (aka Detective Olivia Benson) on the set of *Law and Order: SVU*. As a longtime fan of the show, Detective Benson was one of my favorite characters of all time. To say that I was excited was an understatement.

The client, Kellie Giddish (aka Detective Rollins), told me that Marishka was a Wonder Woman aficionado. Kellie also brought her young superhero obsessed son to see the performance, so the stakes were high and my audience was going to be particularly discerning.

Wonder Woman was a hit. Marishka was as beautiful as she was kind and I got a thumbs up from the 3-year-old ace. Kellie took my photo and put it on her Instagram page. Not only was this seen by my friends and family back home who followed her online, but Wonder Woman helped me make my rent which was due the next day. Bonus, with the money left over, May Wilson got a new dress. Moral of the story: a day job doesn't have to be a drag, it can be awesome.

My publicity photo for BurlesQ at Alexis Park Las Vegas

8 TOOLS OF THE TRADE

You still want to be a ventriloquist after reading the last chapter. Good. Now let's get to how you can be the best ventriloquist you can be at the level you choose, whether it be superstar, small scale or somewhere in between.

The first way to become the best ventriloquist you can be is to do ventriloquism, period. This is the only surefire way to perfect your craft. Perform whenever and wherever possible, whether it's for friends, family, office parties, church functions, open mic nights, amateur nights or whatever booking comes your way. John Pizzi gave this piece of advice to me when I was a young vent, "Take every gig that comes your way. As a matter of fact, I recommend starting at kids' parties and working your way up."

I agree everyone should start out performing for kids or at least do it a handful of times. Children have a reputation for being a tough audience and it is often because their innocence coupled with their station in life makes them exceptionally honest. They will let you know not only where your skills stand, but also their imaginations are incredible and this alone will bring your ventriloquism to a whole new level.

In entertaining children, some vents discover that not only do they fall in love with making kids smile, but they want to make this their prime focus. Even those like myself who do not exclusively entertain children have found these lessons made them stronger in entertaining adult comedy club audiences or casino crowds. Any time and any place you step onstage strengthens your ventriloquial muscles.

If you are a vent performing for children for any reason, Mark Wade has this piece of advice, "You really have to like children. And a lot of people think of children as little adults, and they are not." (Mark Wade also wrote *Kidshow Ventriloquism*, which I highly recommend.)

To perform, you need to know where to find gigs. At first, because you are not yet established, you will have to pound the pavement seeking stage time. These opportunities can be found in in local publications and websites, entertainment trades such as *Backstage*, *Playbill* and *Broadway World*, Facebook groups or even Craigslist. If you put on a great show, there is also the old fashioned word of mouth that can not only get you rebooked, but can get you other bookings elsewhere. Throw your hat (and your puppet's hat) in the ring whenever possible.

With each show you do, not only will you get to know

yourself as a ventriloquist, but you will get to know your market. Once you decide what your market is, then you will know where and how to zero in on particular gigs and how to tailor your act accordingly.

There are some vents who work clean, doing the family and church show circuit. They can also do cruise ships and corporate events making a decent amount of money. However, these gigs often not only have language restrictions, but content restrictions because they are either geared towards a family audience or there is an HR department involved. While this path is lucrative, many vents find the constraints artistically unsatisfying.

Another route is the comedy club route. You can keep your freedom to do the act you want for the most part and you are more likely to get radio and TV appearances down the line; therefore, you are more likely to get known. While it is more artistically satisfying, it does not pay nearly as well. (Singular radio and TV appearances rarely pay, but are used to drum up more work and this means more marketing on your end.)

A recommendation an agent gave me early on was to strike a balance between the two worlds. Not only do you have to engage your creativity more by not using four letter words, but you can make money and have the freedom to express yourself at the comedy clubs. Many big name acts have done this and found success and happiness. Over the years, this has folded into the best recipe for me too. The journey is all about balance.

Another way to find your voice and make money is street performing. Not only don't you have to rely on a venue for stage time, but depending on the day and the foot traffic, you can also make some money, too. As a teen, The Late Otto Petersen was a fixture in Washington Square Park. In a tale that is still told today, the young Otto was performing with George when John Lennon walked by. The Beatle said, "Here is a dollar-fifty, a dollar for you and fifty cents for George."

The point of the story is you never know who is going to see you and street performing is an easy way to cultivate your own opportunities. A few years back, May Wilson and I scored a summer job busking in Brooklyn for a flea market. We were hired because we were quirky, outrageous and appealed to the hipster demographic. The opportunity let us not only break in new jokes, but we made good money in tips on top of the minimum salary we were already paid. One sweltering afternoon, a young man with a handlebar mustache and camera approached May and me. He asked to take our picture and we gave him permission. (May wanted to be photographed alone, I had to beg to stand next to her.)

I struck up a convo with the photographer. Fresh and heartbroken from the recent breakup with my former fiancé, I revealed this happened because he didn't understand my commitment to my vent and felt threatened by my goals. The young man sympathized. While he already had a girlfriend (darn because he was cute), she didn't understand why he had to carry his camera everywhere he went.

The story still has a happy ending though. A little over a year later, I got a call from a production company doing a show called *My Strange Addiction* and they had heard my story from the young man with the camera who happened to have a friend that worked in casting. The show, which has made me a tad controversial among some vent purists, got me a lot of exposure and opened up doors. This was all because I spent a summer busking for hipsters. (Yes, I love *Portlandia*.)

On the other hand, busking can be concerning because of safety issues as you are dealing with strangers who are capable of anything. Nigel Dunkley and Cindy Hot Chocolate, who went viral as a result of busking, can be seen performing regularly in the New York City subway. Nigel offers this advice to young vents who want to cut their teeth that way in regard to the different types of audiences that one might encounter on the street, "Be positive and they will be positive. Be aware of your surroundings and always read your vibe."

An added note about busking, depending on where you do it, you may need to apply for a permit. Without a permit you can be fined. If you are interested in busking, go to your city hall for more information on what is needed to get you the proper credentials.

If you get good enough at the local level, you might get the chance to take your show on the road. Not only will you see new cities, but you will be exposed to audiences whose tastes differ from your home crowd. These experiences can be unnerving, but a bad show isn't a disaster; it's a learning experience. Over time, these shows will make you stronger as you turn into the ventriloquist you were always meant to become.

In the event the idea of being on the road is appealing, it will work in your favor if you are a licensed driver. You will be an asset whether it's a headliner who needs a ride or a group of performers needing transportation. Your wheels make you a go-to and it will be a chance to secure a guest spot and showcase for club owners and bookers who might not otherwise get to see you. Not only can you possibly get more regular road work, but if you impress your passenger/headliner, a consistent opening gig. These credentials and this stage time will not only strengthen your vent act, but make you more attractive to those who want to book you.

Be aware initially road gigs will not be enough to live on so again, don't drop out of school or quit the day job. On a road show, there is an emcee, feature, headliner and potential guest spot. Here is a better explanation of each:

Emcee: First comic up of the evening. Usually green and has been in the game a year or two. They warm the audience up and keep the energy going between the acts. Customarily they do 10 minutes up front, sometimes including crowd work.

Guest Spot: Also, a newer comic and can be someone who works for the club, or is mentored by the feature or headliner. This comic is looking to get experience, and usually does anywhere from five to seven minutes.

Feature: The opening act for the evening. This is a comedian who has been doing comedy for a few years and they are starting to get their sea legs outside of their perspective city. A feature usually does between 25-35 minutes.

Headliner: The so called star of the evening, the headliner is a more established comedian who has a few TV credits to their name. A headliner usually does between 45-60 minutes.

Road gigs are an exciting way not only to become a better ventriloquist, but also to network with more established comedians. Be cautioned though, road gigs can cost money between gas, tolls and at times a hotel room that will not be provided. Gaining experience might mean losing money. While the acts at time split a hotel room three ways, it is still an out of pocket expense. Before you take a road gig, budget the cost and use Google Maps. Pursue dreams, not debt.

An upside of the road is it is a chance to build camaraderie and a support network. This career is a marathon and not a sprint. Today you might be in the trenches, but tomorrow a performer you met once upon a time in your travels might have an opportunity where a ventriloquist is needed and will know to mention your name. When the time comes to repay the favor do it. Teamwork makes the dream work.

Anytime you are offstage, whether you are working locally or on the road, continue to build that sought after professional support network. Do not just seek out peers, but seek out mentors as well. Many times, a newbie vent feels intimidated to approach older vents as if they are a nuisance. This could be farther from the truth.

Steve Hewlett was mentored by the late Keith Harris, who's status was so legendary he performed at Buckingham Palace for the first birthday parties of both Prince William and Prince Harry. When the young Steve asked the older vent to mentor him, he remembers being scared, but also being pleasantly surprised that that Keith willingly and excitedly took on a new charge. Steve Hewlett says, "I like mentoring younger vents. I remember when I was mentored and I want to pay it forward."

Here's another reason why you should approach older vents, mentoring you makes them even more excited about vent and helps keep the art form alive for the next generation. However, even older vents, especially those with established careers, are still cultivating their support networks. So, in mentoring you, as their mentee you are now a part of their offstage support network. (HA! HA!)

You might wonder where you can connect with other vents. You can meet them online in Facebook as well as ventriloquism and puppetry meet-up groups too. In puppetry meet-up groups, you won't just meet ventriloquists, but other kinds of puppeteers too. This is not only an opportunity to connect, but an opportunity to continue to sharpen your tools. Puppeteers have advice for vents that is not only helpful when it comes to synch and other tools to strengthen your craft, but also workshops and castings where a ventriloquist might be needed.

Through meetups, you will discover that all forms of puppetry are related. These groups gave me an opportunity to become proficient in different forms aside from ventriloquism such as hand and rod, full body and Balinese shadow puppetry. These tools not only make seeking employment in show business easier, but have gotten me more wonderful people in my support network, but most importantly, have made me a better ventriloquist.

There are also live events to meet other ventriloquists, such as ConVENTion. While cost might be an issue, there are scholarships available to vents who demonstrate willingness, talent and financial need. Not only is this a chance to get to know others in the community, but to learn about the onstage and offstage workings of what it takes to make vent your career. Money, time away from work and time away from home might be a factor, but remember you are investing in yourself and your future.

As you build your act, get stage time, and cultivate a support network, you will now need a website, too. This is important because you will come up under search engines under the term "ventriloquist." Having a website not only establishes you as being legitimate, but it is also real estate on the World Wide Web.

Additionally, a website is a one stop shop for people who want to hire you and they can get to know all about you, your puppets, and the kind of shows you do. When building a website, make sure it is representative of you and your brand; so, as you build it, know your market.

It is important that your website look good. If you have the funds but fear you lack visual imagination, hire someone to design and maintain your website. In the event funds are an issue, a graphic design student might do it as a favor in exchange for portfolio. If you are a vent with kids, there have been instances where children of the performers not only design but maintain the website for their parent's profession. This might sound ludicrous, but the generation coming up is always ahead of the curve on the latest technology and could create a surprisingly hip website.

If you are good with design but lack the funds, WIX is an excellent web development service and is a relatively cheap. Many performers not only use this service, but have websites that help book them work all the time.

Whether you or someone else designs your site, make sure it is as clean and easy to navigate as possible. Casting people and bookers do not have the time or energy to figure out how to work your site. Having a website that's clear and concise alone will move you up on the list for possible hires in any opportunity.

On your website, you will need a headshot of you, as well as one of you and your figure. Headshots can be very expensive and many of the best headshot photographers start at least $500. If this is not feasible, often times an art student will do them for a discount rate or in exchange for you being a part of their portfolio.

Your headshot should capture both you and your figure, and should be an accurate representation of your act. The temptation of any newbie in the business is to try to post a "glamour shot." Unless this is the angle of your vent act, I advise against it. This will work against you when you show up at a professional audition or booking looking different than your photo. Bookers and casting people also know this trick and will quickly regard you as a rank amateur.

However, do look your best when photographed, and have a few different looks for you and your figure so there are several options to pick from when the shoot is over. Pro-tip: Do not wear busy patterns as they are distracting.

Due to the costly nature of launching a show business career, many vents will fear not having headshots at all and settle for mediocre ones. Do not do this. Industry people will not only see that you are broke and desperate, but they will conclude you are sloppy. They will respond in kind by hiring someone else. No headshot is better than a bad headshot; remember that one good headshot does more than twelve bad ones.

Your website also should have a bio so that people who want to hire you can know a little about you. This information includes your background, what got you into vent, training if any, and a list of venues at which you have appeared. The more you accomplish, the more you should update your bio section. Your bio needs to end with what you are working on currently and your future goals.

On a tab next to your bio, have a calendar and list the venues where you are appearing. This is not only so your followers can see you and your puppets live, but so that industry people can see you live.

Next to the engagement link tab you should have a resume. This should list your professional experience whether it's club dates, theatre shows or revues you have appeared in and TV appearances you have made.

Another thing to include on your resume are classes and workshops you have taken. This can include a BFA or MFA in performance or performance related, an ongoing acting class, workshops/classes at ConVENTion or other puppetry meet-ups, workshops with casting people or other education you might feel might be of interest and importance. Industry people not only value an education, but they are attracted to talent that is always growing, sharpening their skills, and investing in themselves.

A note about your bio and resume, do not fall into the temptation to "pad" your credentials. This ends in disaster for several reasons. First, a credential-padder gets an opportunity and does not have the experience they say they do, thus bombing or costing the production time and money. Second, the booker/casting director was familiar with the project the credential padder claims to have appeared in and knows it's a lie. Third, the booker/casting director worked on the project the credential padder has claimed to have appeared in and knows it's a lie. Don't make yourself the topic of conversation for all the wrong reasons. I know it sounds like common sense, but I have seen people do it far too many times, and to say it ends badly is a gross understatement.

I get that you might be at the beginning of your journey and might be self-conscious about your lack of experience, but don't fall into that trap. Industry people know a performer at the beginning of their journey will have limited experience. They will also appreciate your honesty, and it will make them more likely to give you an opportunity as well as mentor and nurture your talent.

Your website should include clips of you performing ventriloquism. This footage can include internet skits, live performances, or television clips. Only put up the videos up that showcase you best. No reel is better than a bad reel.

Last but not least, your website should include contact information as well as links to your social media. When contacting you personally, many vents have an email address or a contact form, but make sure the contact form is easy to use and linked to your email. A contact form not linked to an email for any reason can result in missed bookings. Make sure your inbox is always cleaned too. An email that bounces back could mean a decision maker bounces from you to another candidate.

As an aside about social media, it has become an online thought box for the world. It is okay to talk about your feelings and have opinions. However, avoid getting into conflict with people, engaging in flame wars with people you disagree with or going to a skree when you are having a particularly bad day. I know this sounds like the obvious, but many people have fallen into this quicksand and it has cost them professional opportunities.

Talent is a part of the puzzle, but show business is two words; art is extra. People who hire talent want you to do a good job, but also want to avoid someone who will do something to put their job in jeopardy. There is an old saying in show business, "No one has ever gotten fired for saying no."

Now let's talk about who will look at your website and hire you. Here are a few industry terms you should know:

Agent: Gets talent jobs whether it's club dates, personal appearances, film or TV work. Takes anywhere from 10-15 percent commission.

Booker: Buys talent for comedy clubs and other smaller rooms. Typically works with agents and managers.

Buyer: Books talent for bigger venues like performing arts centers, casinos and fairs. Typically works with agents and managers.

Casting Director: Scouts talent for theatre, stage revues, film and TV. Typically corresponds with agents and managers.

Manager: Counsels/molds an act on their brand and

how to market themselves in the industry. They help their acts get agents and steer them towards bookers, buyers and venues that will fit their act. Managers typically take 15-20 percent fee of your gross earnings.

Getting an agent/manager is very difficult since many take clients through referral only. This is why it is important to keep emailing, looking for opportunities and getting yourself out there. That being said, a more senior member of your support network can point you to the way of good representation through referral, and this is why that support network is important. Additionally, that same support network can vet a possible representative to let you know whether or not they are legitimate. (*How To Make It As An Actor* by K. Callan has more information about all this, as well as the actor guilds, such as SAG-AFTRA and Equity.)

Life is very doable without an agent in a smaller market and at the beginning it is very doable in NYC, but not so doable in LA. Even with an agent or a manager, you must always be working and marketing yourself, because at the end of the day they have other clients and as K. Callan writes, "You can't expect someone to do a hundred percent of the work when they are getting ten percent of the pay." This means writing, practicing, performing, pursuing opportunity and taking classes.

Once a month, drop your representative a line about future club dates, revues you are currently a part of, TV appearances you made, classes you are taking and anything else you are doing to develop yourself professionally. You will not be your rep's only act. This action will this ensure you don't get lost in the shuffle, but it will move you to the top of the pile when opportunities come along. Agents and managers like a proactive performer. Not only does it show you are taking charge of your career, but they will be excited to advocate for someone who is a go getter.

A word about agents and managers. Show business is a business built on the dreams of hopefuls and unfortunately there are many vultures who prey upon these hopefuls. On the other hand, there are plenty of wonderful agents and managers who care deeply not only for the ethics of their profession, but for the clients they represent. These people often have their cellphones tethered to their sides, and forego sleep to in order to fight for their client so that they reach their goals. Knowing who is who can be difficult.

If you have questions of legitimacy, there are professional associations that you can contact. One is National Conference of Personal Managers (www.NCOPM.com). Not only does NCOPM vet their membership very carefully, but they care about making sure talent knows what is and isn't ethical when it comes to a representative. You can also contact SAG-AFTRA, as well as Actor's Equity.

In the event that someone requests money in exchange for representation, in the words of NCOPM president Clinton Ford Billups Jr., "Go to the mall, get the best pair of running shoes available and run as fast as you can."

This certainly pertains mainly to young women, but men and

nonbinary people can fall victim too. If someone demands sex in exchange for club dates or representation, this is not only bad business practices, but it is illegal. Report them to the police. Sexual coercion is a form of sexual assault and no one at any level has the right to do that to you. Many have caved to these pressures out of fear of not having a career. These predators lie and say that if these hopefuls don't do as they please, they will make sure they never work. This is manipulation and while they are free to threaten to ruin your career, you pressing criminal charges will deservedly put them out of business. Reporting them doesn't just make the industry safer for you, it makes it safer for everyone.

If you are meeting a representative you do not know, it is okay to bring a male friend or partner. In the event the presence of your friend or partner makes the rep feel uneasy, then you know to pass on working with them. However, if the rep understands your need to bring a friend and vet him, he not only will be respectful of your talent, but mindful of the obstacles talent in this business unfortunately face.

While being a working performer is great, you should be one in the safest, most constructive way possible. Remember you don't have to compromise yourself or your safety for an opportunity; there will always be another streetcar. It is your career at the end of the day and you write your own story. You pull your puppet's strings, but you also pull your own.

This is May Wilson and I am perfectly comfortable working the casting couch. (Okay, it's official, I am no longer leaving my laptop open when May is in the room.)

On the set of ABC's "What Would You Do?" with puppet May Wilson

9 PERFORMING ON TV

As a ventriloquist, you see your favorite vents on TV and dream of that being you someday. Or perhaps you have been doing gigs for some time and want to take your act to the next level, which means further recognition and visibility. You might be wondering, "Where do I even start?"

When working on camera, I will tell you the same thing I told you about performing ventriloquism: Do it whenever possible. If you have no experience, an on camera acting class might be a good investment. While it won't be focused on ventriloquism, you will learn technique, how to slate, where to look and what to do in an audition. Most of the time, instructors in these classes have been or are currently working professionals. They also will teach you how to prepare and use your craft best on set.

Another starting place to get on camera experience is producing your own Internet videos. Not only is this fun, but you can sharpen your writing skills by crafting your own scripts and ideas. You can shoot and edit on your phone. This will be a chance to get feedback from not only other vents, but anyone who also sees the video. (Yes, you will get trolls, but this is good because it means people are watching.) The good thing about the Internet is you can be discovered by anyone anywhere in the world all while building a fan base.

Posting videos on YouTube, TikTok or Instagram won't just establish you as a ventriloquist, but can be a way to go viral. Not only will these videos put you in front of a lot of eyeballs, but it will be a way for agents and managers to find you, too. In turn, this means being pitched for film and TV opportunities.

Even if your videos don't go viral, many casting directors often look at online videos when they need to scout for talent. A video you posted today might mean a life changing phone call tomorrow. (I have booked several television appearances this way.)

If your community has a public access station, this might be a way for you to cut your teeth at hosting your own regular show. Access stations offer free classes to residents who want to get into television production; use of the editing suite is free as well. You'll produce your own content and grow a fan base. Many access stations also have a YouTube channel, too.

I am a champion of public access because it changed this vent's world because I did a local access show as a teen.

Storytime With April and Friends, where I read stories with my sidekick Sweetie Pie, a five year old clown, was broadcast in 36 states, six countries and on the World Wide Web, which was then in its infancy.

With *Storytime* I created my own vehicle. Generating press, I got the interest of agents and managers, even getting representation from an agency in my hometown. It also showed the admissions committee at NYU's Tisch School of the Arts that I was a self-stater, giving me a ticket out of my small town and into New York City. My freshmen year of college, *Storytime* was featured in the New York City edition of *TV Guide.*

Storytime did not make me a big star, but was a building block. It introduced me to people who not only gave me professional advice, but at this very moment are still guiding my career.

Another way to gain on camera experience is through low budget and student films. While these shoots are sometimes less than ideal as you are working with a director who has little to no experience, these too are building blocks. That beginning director today might be a big name tomorrow and this might mean more future on camera work for you.

That film you thought of as "no budget" could also shine at festivals, opening doors to distribution and on to streaming platforms. This exposure could also lead to other on camera opportunities.

Student films and low budget castings can be found in

Backstage, Craigslist, your local trades or college bulletin boards in the theatre and film departments. Some of the trades have an online database where you can register by posting your headshot and resume. This will not only make your talent known to people looking to cast, but when Google searches for ventriloquists, this will be another entry for you making you and your figure more legit.

If you want to work in broadcast and film, it is important to know about SAG-AFTRA, the union that protects film, television and radio talent. Union jobs ensure you get decent wages, but if you work enough you become eligible for residuals, healthcare and a pension.

Now you are wondering how to get into the union. Answer: you need to get a union job. It sounds like an *Alice in Wonderland* riddle. Well welcome to show business. However, look on TV, the actors you see have done it and you can do it too.

The first way is to do three "extra" jobs and to collect the vouchers. Once you get three vouchers, you are known as a "Must Join." At the end of each day on set, make sure you collect your vouchers. It is easy to forget because not only are shoot days long, but many times those working behind the scenes are more tired than you are. Be polite anyway, not only will it get you your much needed vouchers, but that production assistant might be a big name director.

In order to get extra jobs, register at your local casting agency that books extras. Make sure you let them know you are a ventriloquist. It will be helpful for them to have a variety act that they didn't previously have on file, but there are a surprising number of projects that you might be eligible for.

If they have you on file, you might be eligible for a Taft-Hartley. This happens when they cannot find a union person with the special skill they are seeking to play a feature, supporting, or starring role. A Taft-Hartley will give you enough points to join the union on that job alone.

In case you are wondering, I joined SAG-AFTRA via Taft-Hartley. If you are a ventriloquist, I would advise joining in that way. Variety acts are very specialized, and it is less likely they will find another union vent. Going this route will take a little longer to get union membership, but is less of an arduous process than long days on set and collecting vouchers from a tired production assistant.

To join the union, it currently costs $3000.00. You can pay upfront, but if you don't have the money to do so the union has a loan program through The Actors' Federal Credit Union.

Once you are a member, you will pay dues twice yearly based on how much you are working. Even if you are not working, I recommend being up to date on your dues, which makes you not only eligible for union work, but also union benefits, industry workshops and disaster resources if you need them. (SAG Foundation and Actors' Fund are wonderful by the way.)

Once you join the union, you cannot work non-union unless

you want to be penalized. Join when it makes sense and you are ready, willing and able to pursue television opportunities and have the tools of the trade to do so.

As you grow your wings and have the tools to be in front of the camera performing with your puppet, let's talk about some of the shows where the eyeballs of viewers might see you. For some you will need a union card and others are nonunion. (Check with your agent, managers, or support network for these particulars. This could be another very long book in itself.)

Late-night TV talk shows are one wonderful way to get seen. Considered the brass ring for comedians and variety acts, you will need seven minutes of clean material. Your set, before you perform it, will have to be okayed by several producers as the TV executives. This is because they have to appease product sponsors. Have the ability to work clean as TV bookers will turn away comedians who don't, even if they are funny.

In order to book a late-night talk show, you need an agent and/or personal manager. Late-night producers will attend showcases, but all of those acts have representation and late-night bookers do not take unsolicited materials.

If you are pursuing a late-night show booking, know that while it is still a prestigious, they do not book as many comedians as they once did. While it is not impossible to be booked, it is less of a market than it used to be.

A second way to get on television are daytime talk shows

that have a segment showcasing talent. These spots have never been as frequent as late-night talk shows, but could be a nice way to get exposure. Just like late-night spots, they are procured through an agent or manager. However, every once in a while there might be a listing in one of the trades looking for talent, so these are a little easier to book.

Your set will have to be squeaky clean-even more so than it would for late-night television. While these opportunities are often non-union, having a union card will not exclude you. Before you take the opportunity, watch the show and make sure it is right for you and your act. Both late-night and daytime television opportunities will not pay you to appear, but they will open doors to club owners, casting directors and anyone looking to hire variety acts

If you are coming from out of town to appear on one of these shows, the network will pay for your airfare and hotel. Keep in mind the most you could be in town in a day or two. Be cautioned, even if you travel to do the show, you might not appear. If a major news story occurs, you might be bumped. However, your appearance will be rescheduled. (There's no business like show business!)

Many vents also get on television through contest reality shows, such as *America's Got Talent*. Several vents won, but it has showcased them for other opportunities in Hollywood, Las Vegas and beyond. These shows often air on major networks during prime time and get you more eyeballs than daytime and late-night combined. Talent show contests can also lead to further appearances on late-night shows and daytime talk shows for talent, too.

I will caution you though, there are major drawbacks to talent show contests of any kind. Just like late-night and daytime TV, they are non-union. While they will pay for your hotel stay, unfortunately in some cases, you will be responsible for your own airfare. The appearance will be nonpaid, and you will not be paid for your time away from home or your support gig either. Depending on how far you make it on the show, this could take up days, weeks or months of your time. Bookings might come as a result of your appearance, but they might not come for months afterward depending on when the show airs; so, your fifteen minutes of "fame" could make you experience a financial windfall.

In order to be seen by producers let alone judges, you will have to be pre-screened for an official audition. Most of the acts who are seen, let alone selected, have representation. Cattle calls are done for B-roll footage as a way to make the casting look fair to give the appearance of people being "discovered." Many times, those who show up for the cattle call do not see the producers.

There have been instances where the show's producers will pay to craft a puppet ahead of time and actively scout a vent to do said pre-scripted act. Your artistic freedom is not only in jeopardy, but you might not be able to do your own act at all.

While getting the go ahead to see the producers might seem

like good news, this is not always the case. Sometimes an act is moved ahead only to be humiliated, and given the X to create the further illusion that the competition is "fair."

If this is something that still interests you, do a lot of research first. Make sure the casting people go through your agent or manager, because your representative will know what questions to ask. If you don't have representation, tap your support network to see if they appeared or know anyone who has appeared, and ask what their experience on said show was. Use this information to decide whether you want to proceed.

The upside of televised competitions, even if you make the B-roll, is that it is still a TV credit. May Wilson and I made the B-roll waiting in line for *Last Comic Standing 5*. It was it a TV credit we used, but it helped launch us out of barking (passing out fliers for stage time) and into guest spots at clubs and on the road. I also got help from another comic waiting in line with the punchline of a joke I was struggling with and it is now one of my best bits. So, if you have the time, a warm jacket and a mug of hot coca, why not wait in the cold with your vent figure?

Another plus to those shows is that although the network controls them, it doesn't mean that you can't take risks. On *Britain's Got Talent*, Steve Hewlett, unknown to Simon Cowell or any of the other judges, unveiled a Simon Cowell puppet and that of his ex-girlfriend Sinetta. The segment not only was well received by the audience, but Simon had no choice but to reward Steve's bravery by passing him to the next round. Although Steve didn't win, he has gotten many, many bookings off of that clip.

Then there are the reality contest shows like *The Bachelor* and *Survivor*. While your ventriloquist act will not be the focus of the show, it might be your hook to casting directors and make you appealing to a television audience. This exposure will be a chance to build your fan base.

While these shows are non-union, the upside is they are easier to get on. You will be paid for your airfare, travel and get a flat rate for your time.

Usually casting notices for these projects will be on Facebook or other groups and you will not need an agent or manager to submit a tape. Getting a spot on these shows is often easier than late-night shows, daytime shows and talent contest shows.

Before you shoot your audition tape, a big downside is you will be cut off from the outside world during the competition meaning you cannot communicate with family or friends. Not only will your every move be filmed, but you will sign a contract allowing the network and production company to do whatever they want with your footage.

If you are a fan of one of these shows and it has always been your dream, I say go for it but know the risks versus reward ahead of time. Have a plan on how you want to leverage the opportunity. Talk it over with your support network ahead of time and get their feedback. They might know a few pitfalls, or they might have some ideas so you can get more momentum for your vent career if you are chosen.

Of course, there are the shows featuring "odd people" like *My Strange Addiction.* I made my debut as the "girl addicted to puppets." As I talked about in the previous chapter, I had been scouted while street performing. During my interview, I told the casting people ventriloquism was the deal breaker with my ex. While the story is far more complicated and I said this then and even now, this is the narrative the network ran with. (They took some creative license.)

The appearance got me not only on TLC and OWN, but other television shows, too. It made me controversial in the vent community, but on the other hand, it got several of my fans to finally urge me to write this book. (Good old risk versus reward.)

My Strange Addiction not only helped me build a fan base, but led to the chance for May and me to star in a low budget horror film, show dates in NYC, legit acting and modeling sans puppet, making my own music, and May Wilson and I becoming talking heads online.

These appearances put me on the radar of casting directors who needed a ventriloquist, and led to an appearance with May Wilson on *What Would You Do?* (ABC's hidden camera show). Not only was this a union appearance that still pays me residuals, but helped me land a manager and a steady gig in Las Vegas.

Then of course, there are television specials, and vents have shined there, such as Jeff Dunham's, whose *Very Special*

Christmas Special was the most watched in Comedy Central history. Taylor Mason and his crew are regulars on *Dry Bar Comedy,* which are specials for a family orientated audience.

Comedy specials a chance to make money through worldwide distribution, but it is a chance to showcase to bigger bookers and network brass. Through his successful TV specials, Jeff Dunham scored his own show on Comedy Central.

Many vets are starting to self-produce their own television specials, myself included. *Broke and Semi-Famous* was out of my own pocket and I skimped out on the non-essentials for months which made life interesting. Not only did I put together a long set, but I learned the basics of marketing and streaming. *Broke and Semi-Famous* did not end up on a major platform, it aired once on Love TV in Finland which got me more coverage outside of the United States. I also had other vents downloading the special, which established my place in the community.

One of these vents was Darren Carr in Australia, to whom I had written a fan letter to as a kid. It was exciting because it felt like my journey and the stress of producing my own special was worth it. (The clips from my special also have helped my manager leverage me for other film and TV opportunities.)

While I don't regret producing my own special, it was more work than I was ready for. So, if you are going to go this route, make sure you plan ahead, have the funding and a lot of support. Tap into your support network to see if anyone has done this before, because nothing is worse and more frustrating than reinventing the wheel.

Lastly, there is episodic television and film, which you need to have union membership to do. Not only does episodic TV especially pay you a decent regular paycheck, but as a bonus with that and films, when they air reruns, you can collect residuals. (YAY!!!!)

The challenge with ventriloquists in situation comedy, episodic television and film is how do they honor their craft and fulfill the creative demands of the medium. Jay Johnson starred with sidekick Bob Campbell on *Soap,* an ABC sitcom in the late 1970s. He and director Jay Sandrich came up with the following rules to help Bob not only become real and lifelike, but to keep the illusion going:

1. Bob was never to be referred to as the dummy, but Bob or Bob Campbell at all times.
2. Bob was credited as Bob Campbell in the credits.
3. It was always a two-shot to keep the truth of the ventriloquism going
4. When Bob was working, he was out of the trunk and when he was done, he was put away.

While you do not have to employ these, I have found those rules helpful as a working vent on any set anywhere. It keeps the truth of your vent character as a part of the story, but it also makes network and television execs, who are seldom creative, use their imagination and more excited about working with a ventriloquist.

As you start to book television work and see your name in lights, remember at the end of the day you are still a ventriloquist. There is still another routine to be crafted, still another joke to be told, still another brass ring to be won.

If you are fortunate enough to be on TV, don't rest on your laurels and make your ego your amigo, feeling that you never have to write or perfect your craft because that is the farthest thing from the truth. Luck and timing equal success and once that opportunity comes, you need to work harder than ever before. Fame is fleeting and there is no substitute for having the goods. When the lights are on, you and your partner on your arm need to be the best you can be and make the crowd laugh. You both will not only keep it fun, but it will give you longevity in the business of show.

An April Anecdote

It's a warm June day, perfect for May Wilson and I to street perform at The South Street Seaport. What the unsuspecting eye doesn't know is that we aren't just any street performers, but we are filming for *What Would You Do?,* the ABC hidden-camera show. Behind the mic, May is slinging out some callous comedy. She says to an itinerant woman sleeping on a park bench, "Hey homeless lady, why don't you get yourself some dignity and self-respect!"

A doorman on his cigarette break does not see the humor in this situation. Springing into action, he says, "Hey, stop making fun of the homeless lady!" Smoke is metaphorically and physically coming out of his nostrils, but we can't blow our cover until the production crew appears. I point to May Wilson, "It's not me, it's her."

He says, "Well, when the cops come they are going to arrest both of youz!" Right on cue, John Quinones and the camera crew appear and say to the doorman, "Hi, we are with *What Would You Do?!*"

The homeless woman reveals she isn't what she appears either because she's actually an actress. In an added O. Henry twist, it turns out that she is far from indigent, as she took a $200 car service to the location that morning.

Moral of the story: Call out rotten puppets because you might be a hero on national TV.

In support of unemployed entertainment workers

10 DEALING WITH THE UNEXPECTED

There is a famous showbiz saying, "The show must go on." The etymology of this expression comes from the days of the circus. Animals fell ill, an acrobat got injured, a horn player ran off with a girl he met in a town or a clown just quit. You name the crisis, it was happening. The circus folk knew that unlike a department store, they would not be open indefinitely, their run in said town was limited and the magic of live performance is lightning in a bottle; it happens only once when conditions are set and cannot be repeated.

Cancelling the show was an option for the circus folk, it meant they wouldn't get paid. Ever respectful of those who bought tickets, they did the only thing they knew how to do; they put on the best show they could without letting the offstage drama ruin the night.

This doesn't just apply to the circus, but ventriloquism too. For instance, you book a gig thinking it is going to be one thing, but it ends up being something quite different. When

I was 15, I was performing with my Groucho Marx figure at the local nursing home. I arrived with my puppet in hand and my mom with a camera around her neck, hoping to get snapshots for my future college applications.

The activities coordinator, with a smile, said, "Would you be comfortable playing the memory unit?"

I said yes, not knowing what I was agreeing to, but confident because I had been practicing my venting ever so hard. As we arrived at the memory unit, we were greeted by a woman who had a rain hat, rain boots and an umbrella indoors. This struck me as odd, but I was talking to a puppet; who am I to judge?

The show started, and several of my audience members believed Groucho was real. Yes, they thought he was the real man with the painted mustache and the ever ready cigar and one liner. Suddenly it clicked: Memory unit meant Alzheimer's and dementia!

One woman yelled at Groucho for not making films anymore. Another man asked where his brothers were in earnest. A third woman grabbed Groucho and screamed, "PLEASE TAKE ME WITH YOU! MY CHILDREN PUT ME IN HERE! TAKE ME WITH YOU, I WANT TO GET OUT OF HERE!!!"

The ventriloquist gig I had so looked forward to suddenly turned into a horror show. I was a fifteen year old high school student who watched MTV, read *Seventeen* magazine, barely cleaned her room and was still rather green to the world of vent. To say I was unequipped for any of this was a vast understatement.

As the train was headed off the tracks, the only thing I could do was throw the script for the show I had planned out the window. I got offstage and went from person to person, having Groucho "talk" to them. To my pleasant surprise, it worked and the residents liked the show. It was such a success I got a second booking.

On the car ride home my mom and I celebrated my triumph by laughing and agreeing it would someday be a great story. Years later, I was told by several comedian peers that they admired my "ability to think on my feet." I wanted to say, "Guys, you have no idea..."

I have gotten gigs where a booker who has left out important information that would have been helpful. One well-intended woman who was new to booking live comedy neglected to tell me I was performing for a crowd of deaf people. Next to May Wilson and me would be a sign language interpreter. As an extra plot twist, the interpreter was not only new to interpreting, but had never worked with a vent act before. It was an interesting evening, but luckily the crowd was appreciative.

However, there have been times when the booker left out information and it did not go so smoothly. Once, I played a veteran's home and was not told I would be performing in a detox unit. A man withdrawing from heroin had a violent seizure in the middle of my set and continuing after that was next to impossible. I still finished though, which was all I could do after my set was paused so he could receive medical attention. When I got offstage, a comedian friend of mine put his arm around me and said, "I gotta give you credit, it's pretty tough to follow a seizure."

Another time I was booked to play a retirement home, and they cut the bingo game short for my show. Bingo, which was the big event of the week, was something the residents looked forward to. I was heckled by a 90-year-old woman who not only was angry Bingo was cancelled, but was the reigning champion and sought to double her winnings. My puppets and I had sabotaged her champion streak.

Thinking on my feet, I flipped the script and was able to save myself by having my puppets talk about how much they loved Bingo. When I got offstage the booker said, "Next time I will tell my boss not to cut bingo short." (Ummm, thanks I guess.)

Some gigs are war stories. Funny anecdotes in retrospect, they give you battle scars you remember forever. Stories like these not only give you something to talk about with your peers, but you will discover they might even have a few that could top yours.

Sometimes, a gig with so many mishaps is a chance for ventriloquial growth. A few years ago, I was thinking of leaving the business. I had been dealing with some personal and health issues. While I had some success as a ventriloquist, life was showing me this might not be my ultimate path. An hour after I lamented my misfortune to a close friend, I got a call from a booker looking for a replacement for a ventriloquist who had been suffering a nervous breakdown. Apparently, said ventriloquist was showing up to his gigs without his puppets. (Even when I am mad at her, I still remember to bring May Wilson.)

The booker asked me point blank if I had any experience headlining on the road. I had TV credits under my belt and had headlined plenty in the rooms and clubs of New York, but not on the road. Not sure if vent would be my destiny at this juncture, I decided to tell the truth figuring the worst he could do was close the door in my face. My experience headlining on the road was a whopping zero.

Pleasantly surprised by my honesty, the booker offered me the gig. I went to the club which was in rural Connecticut and did the same vent act I did in New York City. Riding on my TV credits, I thought May Wilson would charm them like she always did. I was wrong; we ate it for 45 whole minutes. (May Wilson insists she was the star and I ruined it.)

After the show, the club owner told me things had to be different the following night. After a rough few months, what little was left of my ego was gone and I felt maybe it was time for me to hang it up; I didn't have the goods. Just as I was ready to tune him out, he revealed he had a background as a Vegas headliner. He offered to help me the next day if I was willing. I said yes.

We talked about crowds outside of NYC and how to play to

the different, older, more suburban demographic. As someone who worked not only with well-known headliners but several vents over the years, he had a lot of ideas on how we were going to better appeal.

The next night was a different story. Not only did I do two good shows (okay the first one was great, the second was alright), but my act went to a different level.

My honesty also helped get me an in with a booker who had more connections for more work and I stopped feeling sorry for myself offstage. I decided I wanted to be a headliner, but I was willing to work as hard as I did before I ever had a TV credit to my name. It became clear vent would be my destiny, but I came to love it more than I ever thought possible. Maybe my pride and ego were bruised, but the growth that happened was worth it.

There are other instances where I have not been as lucky and the booker has not been on my side. One morning, I was doing a show for demons… I mean children… and they were terribly unsupervised by the adults who were supposedly in charge.

During the course of the gig these pint sized imps mouthed off, hit my puppets, hit me and proceeded to run around and scream during my show. I tried everything I could, but having no support from the adults in charge made the situation impossible. When the adult in charge finally decided to crack down, they mouthed off to him. As I was ready to take my money and run as far away as I could, the community director told me what a horrible ventriloquist I was and how I had wasted his time.

It was early enough that I could cash it and it would clear by the end of the day. Just as the money was liquid in my account, I received an email from the community director telling me the entertainment was "not good" and he had to "issue a lot of refunds." In tears, I called my manager who said, "Step over this one and move on. Don't cry, you got paid."

The odds were against me from the start, but the lesson was in the correspondence beforehand. In the emails, the program director was vague about the kind of show he wanted, the ages of the kids attending and tried to haggle me down not once but three times price wise. When I tried to get more information, he wasn't forthcoming.

My gut told me not to take the booking, but a gig is a gig. The lesson here is you don't have to take every booking that comes your way. If you are not comfortable with the correspondence, you can tell the booker the gig isn't for you.

The other lesson from this gig is it gave me a better sense of boundaries. After telling this story to a performer friend who is also a parent they said, "Let me stop you. Hitting your puppets and you is unacceptable. When that starts, you nip that in the bud right away by saying no. If you tell them no and the show will stop if they keep it up, they will listen."

The friend was right. Putting up these boundaries with child audiences not only makes me saner as the ventriloquist, but establishes boundaries makes some of the more rambunctious youngsters respect me more.

Another unexpected with young child audiences is, depending on their age, they are still figuring out the world around them. Due to the fact kids have active imaginations and are exposed to a lot of stimuli, there are times when very young children (ages 2-4) will believe your puppets are real. This has happened to me several times and a few kids have gotten so scared they have cried.

At times like this, it is okay to break from your show and let the kids know it is in fact a puppet. Not only does this help ease their fear, but kids become curious as to how it works and how ventriloquism is done. I have done shows where not only did I do this, but I gave my young audience a vent lesson using their hands. Afterwards, these little vents run up to their parents, attempting to talk without moving their lips. In turn, their parents curse my name. (Or I created the next vent superstar, you never know.)

Then there are hecklers. Yes, if you perform in comedy clubs, especially as a ventriloquist, you will see your fair share. This is why you and your figure need to have a few snappy comebacks. Nothing shuts a heckler down better, especially when they are arguing with a puppet. Actually, the heckler arguing with the puppet not only makes them look foolish, but you have won the night.

Every crowd has a different personality. If you play a resort and have a good Friday or Saturday crowd, Sunday might be laid back and non-responsive. All you can do is go with it and have the best attitude you can. If you have fun, they will have fun.

Other times nothing you do might work and the crowd might nod politely which will confuse you more. Then you find out that they are from another country and don't speak English, but have enjoyed the show.

There are the crowds who have come to party. These include Friday night late shows on the road, bachelorette parties, bachelor parties, birthday parties, girl's nights out and anything in between. In these cases, don't be afraid to flip the script and get rowdy with them. In turn, they will they love you, and these folks will be the first to follow you on social media. This level of flexibility takes time, but in the words of the late Bob Vincent, "This separates an amateur from a pro."

Then there are the gigs you're just dead on arrival and there is nothing you can do. Some night you might be doing a show at a bar and a playoff game is in the next room. TV blaring and cheering filling the air, people don't even notice let alone hear your set. Or it is a laid back bar show and the crowd is not only disinterested, but also the series finale of *The Bachelor* is on the bar TV. Maybe the sound system doesn't work well and people are talking. My favorite are the nights where everything is perfect and suddenly there is a disaster outside like a jumper, a fire, or a shooting. Yes, all these things have happened during shows I have been on.

The only thing to do is to embrace the chaos and use the time wisely. Sometimes you need to treat the gig like an open mic, doing your time and getting more comfortable performing your set with your figure on the stage. If it makes sense, you can jump off the stage, take your puppet, and chat it up with the patrons at the bar. (This was always my favorite.) If all else fails, thank the audience, get offstage, go home, go to sleep and know tomorrow is a new day and a better show is around the corner.

In some instances, all hell is breaking loose, but the good news is, you can still press reset and start again. When I was still quite green in NYC, I was booked on a variety night and got an email from the host that the emcee had cancelled. He wondered if May Wilson and I could fill in as I had experience emceeing on the road. Stoked because I was getting twenty whole dollars, I said yes.

The show was at a queer friendly venue. At that time, aside from gay and lesbians, I didn't know that there was any more variation in the LGBTQ community. When May Wilson did a joke about having a "sex change" (this was back when she was a converted Jerry Mahoney doll), I was met with some very vocal hostility from audience members.

The show had an intermission and I was supposed to do a second set with May. As the audience filed out to go to the restroom, I received a lot of death stares.

I was pulled aside by an audience member whom I will call John. He explained the crowd was mostly trans and nonbinary folks, himself included. John explained the term "sex change" was not only outdated, but offensive to the trans population who have been victims of disproportionate violence over the years. I was stunned, and explained this was my first actual encounter with trans people. My goal was to be entertaining, not an insulting bully to an at risk population. John said, "It's not your fault, someone should have told you."

I got onstage for my second set and broke the cardinal comedy rule, I apologized for offending my audience. May explained this had been her fault, she put the words in my mouth and was drinking when she wrote the joke. The crowd responded by applauding, and the rest of the evening was much smoother.

My efforts were rewarded at the end of the night by the producer who not only paid me the twenty dollars I was initially promised, but gave me an extra twenty as a thank you. I got my first lesson in pronouns, plus I learned that I could be funny without being mean.

I cannot write this chapter without including "acts of God." The acts of God I have experienced are, but were not limited to, my car catching on fire; my bus/plane/train being delayed because of snow or heavy rain; a massive tree falling on the train tracks taking hours to clear; train rerouted because of flooding from hurricane Sandy; powerlines down; my train trapped in the tunnel because of a surprise tornado in Queens; another train delay because of a suicide jumper; and my ride going to the wrong place leaving me stranded in the cold, snow or rain.

In case you experience said cataclysms, have your cellphone fully powered and always carry your charger with you. If catastrophe comes your way, call the booker and be completely honest about what's going on and where you are. Most of the time they will be very accommodating as they are people too and know life happens; their primary concern is the show, so they want to see you are safely there. (As an aside, bookers who have a background as performers are especially understanding and have a few travel horror stories of their own.)

I cannot forget personal calamities. Mine have been ,but are not limited to, having my wallet stolen on the way to a gig; hearing news friends/family members died minutes before stepping onstage; going from a wake to a road date; having my house burglarized and dealing with the NYPD before making a club appearance; dealing with bed bugs that infected my puppets; being in a legal battle with my landlord all day and doing an industry showcase that night; receiving bad medical news before a big show; going through several breakups that I thought were going to destroy me while dealing with demanding bookers; and the list goes on.

Just as my list goes on, so does life. Each time I had to suit up and show up because the audience had paid to see me and my puppets. There were times where it was easier than others, but some of my best sets have been when the world around me was imploding and going to hell. Just like May Wilson, your partner might rub it in a little more, but they have been with you since the beginning.

I would be remiss if I didn't talk about worldwide disaster. Back in 2008, when the market popped, I had been working a ton as a ventriloquist and thought it would last forever. The following spring, the bookings were gone and I could barely get a job in Times Square passing out fliers for a BBQ chain. Rent went from paying itself to McDonalds becoming fine dining.

My mom begged me to give up vent and move home, but I was bound and determined to make this work. I started street performing, hosted an open mic and produced my own one woman shows. While times were dark, the gift of this uncertainty was I was forced to generate my own opportunities. This paid off as work suddenly started to come my way without me even trying. I thought worldwide disaster would never happen again.

WRONG!

After years of a lot of dues paying, my one woman residency, *April Unwrapped*, premiered in Las Vegas in February 2020. Coronavirus came and everything closed, especially casino resort showrooms and theatres. So, all I could do was hope, pray and work on my act because a pity party is ultimately time and potential wasted.

As the world began to open up in late-2020, May Wilson and I headlined as the special guest stars in an all-female revue called *BurlesQ* at Alexis Park Resort Las Vegas. I was one of the few variety acts working in Sin City and the only ventriloquist.

May Wilson and I performed with a 12-foot gap between us and the audience. There was a state-mandated capacity limit in the room with six feet social distancing between the tables. The audience was required to wear face masks, except when they were drinking. There were times when I could not hear them laugh; there were times they were so eager for human interaction that they would talk to May like an audience of small children. Heck, there were times they hadn't been out of the house in months and wanted to party and May Wilson was always down. More than anything, these crowds were very appreciative; it felt good to be in front of a live audience once again.

Each time I stepped on stage, although it was in the midst of a worldwide pandemic disaster, I got stronger. Getting to do this with my life wasn't just a job, it was a gift.

My mantra was not only the old circus adage, but the Freddie Mercury song. Often times, as I drove home having put another show under my belt, May Wilson slept in her trunk and I sang, "The show must go on!"

An April Anecdote

Setting: Las Vegas, 2016. UNLV Cafeteria, one hour before Presidential Debate. It has already been a long day for the credentialed press and everyone is getting pizza before the main event that evening.

Players: April (Ventriloquist/Reporter), Donald J. Tramp (Puppet), Cameraman (Dork, 20s), Chris Matthews (Anchor, MSNBC).

Donald J. Tramp and April, serving as correspondents for the Pulitzer Prize nominated Clyde Fitch Report, are trying to muster their second wind. Cameraman notices a white haired fellow in suspenders and a striped shirt.

Cameraman: There's Chris Matthews. Get a picture!

April, Donald and Cameraman approach Chris Matthews. The visibly tired newsman now has a look of confusion on his face.

April: Chris Matthews! Can I get a picture?

Chris: Yes, you can. But he can't, because I don't like him.

Chris Matthews points to Donald J. Tramp as Donald makes a sad sound. April hands her cellphone to Cameraman who snaps photo. Still confused, Chris Matthews exits.

Donald J. Tramp: If the fake news can bring it, you can bring it too!

Cameraman: You know, the puppet is right

End Scene.

My Opening Night in Las Vegas
April Brucker

11 AFTERWORD

Years ago, in my first semester at NYU, I was feeling very homesick and frustrated. Dropping out of school, moving back home and abandoning my dreams of passion seemed to be the answer. Sandra Bowie, the liaison who handled students in any kind of distress, gave me some advice that changed my life, "Let me tell you what your problem is. You want what you want, and you want it now. A life and a career as an artist are a process and nothing can happen before it's time."

Fast forward. I stayed in school, paid my dues and at times, while it felt dark and uncertain, I trusted the process. The years of hard work culminated into a Las Vegas residency, *April Unwrapped.* My puppets and I had two premiere weekends in Las Vegas. We were well received and I was on my way. Then the pandemic happened and the whole world shut down.

I had friends back in NYC test positive for coronavirus,

some ended up on ventilators and others died. My sister, an ER doctor, was on the front lines in a hazmat suit. We feared not only for her health and safety, but that of her husband and her baby daughter. The shutdowns went for days, weeks, and then months. No one was sure when the world would open and the fate of the entertainment business remained unknown. Maybe my decision to follow my dreams as a professional ventriloquist had been a mistake because the process, so to speak, did not have a contingency plan for worldwide dumpster fire.

I tried to make the best of things by doing Zoom shows. The audience was on mute, so I didn't get any feedback. Denver Goldie and Pat, the house pets, gave me sympathy barks and chirps. Finally, I couldn't take it anymore. At the end of my rope, I told my manager, Clinton Ford Billups Jr., how I felt. That's when, for the umpteenth time, he suggested I write a book on ventriloquism.

Clinton had been suggesting this for years, but I was always too busy with shows, TV tapings, helping to plan my sister's wedding, grad school or whatever other excuse I could come up with. Now, all I had was time; so why not?

During the course of writing *Don't Read My Lips*, I had the opportunity to interview Jay Johnson. After that first year at NYU, I had a chance to see his off-Broadway one man show, *The Two and Only*, at The Atlantic Theatre Company. Jay and his cavalcade of characters were not only entertaining and charming, but he showed me that the sky was the limit with ventriloquism and that I should stick with it and continue to follow my dreams.

The Two and Only made its way to Broadway and would eventually win a Tony. I asked him what it was like being on Broadway and Jay said, "It was a different ball game. I have done comedy clubs and TV, but a one-man show is taking the audience on a journey. This is always about growth." That's when it hit me. The process did have a contingency plan for a worldwide pandemic; it was to dive into the work and trust it more than ever.

During quarantine I worked with monk-like efficiency. My days consisted of me writing *Don't Read My Lips* in the morning and then practicing with my puppets all afternoon. I started to reach new levels with my ventriloquism and joke writing and experimented with new things in the act. Zoom shows soon became a treat for me to show my audiences what I was learning and working on. Writing sessions became a positive way to start my day.

As the world opened up, May Wilson and I stood on a stage four nights a week headlining as the special guest stars in *BurlesQ*, an all-female, classic Vegas revue. While the twenty-five foot gap in front between the stage and the audience felt like the red sea unparted, I always ran the risk of audiences who weren't receptive to ventriloquism. But I got lucky. Not only had I exceeded the expectations of showgoers, but also my own. None of this growth would have happened without the COVID-19 lockdown because nothing truly happens before it's time.

COVID-19 and writing this book made me love ventriloquism again in a way that I didn't think was possible. My advice was so good, I was forced to take it. It re-taught me the lesson that while setbacks hurt, "no" sometimes means "not yet". Post-pandemic, I have recorded guest appearances on a new show on The HISTORY Channel, a network game show and an Amazon TV pilot. I also hosted 12 episodes of "April in Vegas, a streaming TV chat show series produced on location at The English Hotel, a Marriott Tribute Portfolio boutique hotel in the Las Vegas Arts District. After many years, May Wilson and I reunited with our old friend Jerry Springer on NBC's courtroom TV show "Judge Jerry". We told him that we had taken his advice. Jerry graciously replied, "April, you're very talented." So, the good news is that my hard work paid off. The bad news is that I still have more work to do.

In *The Two and Only*, Jay Johnson ends his show by saying that, "You do not choose ventriloquism, it chooses you." So hopefully through *Don't Read My Lips*, ventriloquism has chosen you. If I could leave you with one thing, please know that ventriloquism and life in art is a process. While that process doesn't always give instant gratification, know that it does deliver eventually. May that process always be the force that guides you forward and may your dream of passion always be your rainbow in the dark.

Cheers,

April Brucker
and my Puppet Family

An April Anecdote

Setting: Las Vegas, Alexis Park Resort. BurlesQ performance has just finished and the cast is leaving the building.

Characters: April Brucker (ventriloquist), May Wilson (puppet, not seen, but in suitcase), Audience Member (Woman 40s, waiting for car service in resort lobby).

April walks through the with rolling suitcase. Audience member is waiting for car pickup.

Audience Member: Excuse me, do you know that you were on TV last night?

April: I was?

Audience Member: Yeah, "My Strange Addiction" on TLC. And you really need be nice to May. She's all pent up.

April: I will. Thank you again for coming to the show.

April exits lobby as May speaks from inside the suitcase

May: Ahemmm….. we taped that TV show ten years ago. I was the star then and I am the star now. And you still make me travel in this suitcase. Next time, take me out so I can meet my public!

Moral of the Story: Television is evergreen and puppets are always demanding divas.

ABOUT THE AUTHOR

April Brucker is an American actress, author, comedienne and television personality.

Her television credits include *Entertainment Tonight* (CBS Paramount), *Inside Edition* (King World), *Judge Jerry* (NBC Universal), *The Layover* (Travel Channel), *Let's Make a Deal* (CBS), *My Strange Addiction* (TLC), *Secret Restoration* (The HISTORY Channel), *Today* (NBC), *Videos After Dark* (ABC), *The Wendy Williams Show* (FOX), *What's My Secret?* (MTV), *What Would You Do?* (ABC) and many other network, cable and international TV shows.

The Wrap News - Covering Hollywood described April as "sweet, adorable… with a hint of insanity." VegasNews.com called her "America's foremost female ventriloquist." John Katsilometes, *Las Vegas Review Journal* entertainment columnist said, "She's fun, this one."

Growing up in Bethel Park, Pennsylvania, April spent more than a decade living, acting and performing in New York City at cabarets (Don't Tell Mama, The Duplex, The Metropolitan Room), in comedy clubs (Broadway Comedy Club, New York Comedy Club, Standup New York) and in off -Broadway shows, including "Murdered By The Mob,"

New York's longest running dinner theater production.

In Las Vegas, she has performed at Notoriety Theater, Planet Hollywood Resort & Casino and headlined as the special guest star in the all-female revue "BurlesQ" at Alexis Park Resort. April is the host of "April in Vegas," a streaming TV chat show series produced on location at The English Hotel, a Marriott Tribute Portfolio boutique hotel in the Las Vegas Arts District.

April earned her Bachelor of Fine Arts Degree in Acting at New York University's Tisch School and was awarded a Master of Fine Arts Degree in Creative Writing & Screenwriting from Antioch University Los Angeles. She is the author of several books and is a proud member of SAG-AFTRA.

You can connect with her on Facebook, Instagram, TikTok and Twitter.

More on April at www.AprilBrucker.TV.

INDEX

A

B

C

D

E

F

G

H

I

J

K

L

M

N

O

P

Q

R

S

T

U

V

W

Z

Made in the USA
Las Vegas, NV
18 October 2023